WEALTH

your road map to financial freedom

HIGHWAY

Steve Lawson

PRAISE FOR

WEALTH HIGHWAY

I've worked with Steve for years, and his principles deliver real results for my portfolio. Steve's insights are unmatched. He sees opportunities others miss and turns them into actionable strategies.

-Wade Williams

"The Wealth Highway" is a book that gives a completely new and fresh perspective on investing, one that shows you how to achieve financial independence faster by breaking away from traditional broken methods that keeps us trapped. No matter where you are on your financial journey, this book can help you find and achieve financial independence. You will need to shift your mindset away from the traditional thinking. The secret as explained is to have your money working for you instead of you working for money. If you are ready to change where you're at financially, it is time for you to get on a different road. I would highly recommend you read "The Wealth Highway" because this is the path to true financial freedom.

-Chris Naugle

Founder of PrivateMoneyClub.com and Money School/BYOB

Steve Lawson brings a rare diversity of thoughtfully curated, often unconventional, and hard to find opportunities to the Unbroken Investing group. Paired with the education he provides, investors can best match the right opportunities to their goals and comfort level.

-Linsey K

Steve has a rare combo: sharp on strategy, honest about risk, and genuinely committed to helping people build real passive cash flow. The framework in this book isn't hype—it's a clear, practical playbook for diversification and repeatable decision-making. Using this approach, I discovered dozens of non-traditional ways to grow my wealth and diversify my portfolio, and I came away with a much stronger investing game plan.

 -Michael Lazarenco

I've known Steve for over a decade and witnessed his expertise in investing and financial strategy, especially in real estate and passive income. What distinguishes him is his character—operating with honesty, integrity, and genuine commitment to helping others make sound decisions. In an industry where trust is paramount, Steve demonstrates wisdom and principle. This book will inspire readers to think differently about wealth creation.

 — Andy O'Geare

Steve has been tireless in peeling back the veil that covers investment strategies and opportunities that are either obscure, or only available to people with exceptional means or connections, and making them available to ordinary people like myself.

Steve has provided the education and opportunities for rewards/returns that are possible if you think outside the box and accept a little more risk!

 –Tim Stein

Steve provides a fresh take on investing with impactful concepts that are easy to understand.

–Kevin Kucera

Steve has managed to distill the complex journey of wealth building into a clear, actionable five-level framework. What sets this book apart is the shift from simple budgeting to the sophisticated use of OPM and OPT. By breaking down passive cash flow into sustainable, inflation-indexed stages, he provides a realistic blueprint for anyone looking to transition from a paycheck to true financial sovereignty. This is a must-read for anyone who thinks they don't have the time or capital to start, and we offer it to all IRA Club members starting their self-directed retirement journey.

-Ramez Fakhoury

Vice President of The IRA Club

WEALTH HIGHWAY

WEALTH HIGHWAY

Your Road Map to Financial Freedom

Steve Lawson

WEALTH HIGHWAY

Your Road Map to Financial Freedom

Steve Lawson

ISBN: 978-1-968149-09-3

Joint Venture Publishing

The Millionaire Mentor, Inc.

Printed in the United States of America

DEDICATION

To my wife and children—

the heartbeat behind every mile of this journey.

"Someone is sitting in the shade today because someone planted a tree a long time ago."

- Warren Buffett

TABLE OF CONTENTS

Foreword

Introduction

Chapter 17:

Chapter 18:

About the Author

FOREWORD

Through decades of studying success and stewarding the Think and Grow Rich legacy, I have learned that financial independence is not achieved through chance or enthusiasm alone—it is built through clarity, structure, and disciplined execution. Wealth Highway delivers a practical framework for understanding wealth that goes beyond traditional investing advice. By clearly defining the five levels of financial freedom, this book allows readers to identify exactly where they are in their journey and what is required to move forward with intention.

I have worked alongside Steve Lawson as a business colleague and shared the stage with him at events such as Secret Knock, where ideas are tested in real-world environments. What distinguishes this work is its ability to simplify complex financial concepts while preserving their strategic depth. With a strong emphasis on passive cash flow, diversification, and a refined perspective on wealth, Wealth Highway provides investors with actionable strategies to accelerate progress toward lasting financial independence. For those committed to advancing to the next level, this book offers both clarity and direction.

—Greg Reid

Introduction

"You cannot out-earn poor money management."

That single notion transformed my life.

For years, I believed what many people believe: as long as my income increased, everything would eventually work out. When money was tight, I told myself it was temporary—things would be fine once I earned more.

What I eventually realized is that poor financial decisions don't disappear as income increases. They often get worse.

I've known doctors with fantastic salaries who were drowning financially, and people with modest incomes who quietly attained complete financial freedom. The difference was never intelligence, effort, or luck. It was understanding how money actually works—and more importantly, why wealth matters in the first place.

I don't believe the goal is to "get rich" to impress people, collect possessions, or win some imaginary status game. Wealth is a tool that gives you freedom: to do more of what you love, spend time with people who matter most, and build a life you don't need to escape from. For some, that means travel and adventure. For others, it's being fully present with family, serving a cause they care about, or simply waking up without financial stress. The lifestyle is personal. The freedom is universal.

This book exists because I wish someone had shown me these truths sooner.

I didn't write this as a textbook or step-by-step guide—there are enough of those already, and most overcomplicate things or focus on theory over reality. Instead, I wrote it as a story: a road trip, a series of conversations, a journey most people are already taking whether they realize it or not.

Throughout that journey, I share ideas I learned as a financial advisor over several decades. Some came from my own mistakes. Others from observing what worked—and failed—for hundreds of clients. These aren't just stock market principles or retirement formulas. They're practical concepts about cash flow, mindset, leverage, business ownership, real assets, and time.

Most importantly, this book will challenge you to think differently.

Financial freedom isn't about reaching a magic number or hoping the market cooperates. It's about generating enough consistent passive income to sustain the lifestyle you want—without fear, guesswork, or needing to "die on schedule."

Have you ever felt like you're doing everything right financially but still falling behind? Ever wondered why money feels harder than it should?

If you're ready to learn a better way, I invite you to join this journey.

Read slowly. Think deeply. Be willing to question what you've been taught.

The path ahead may not be what you expected, but it will take you somewhere far better.

CHAPTER 1:

Take the First Step to Financial Freedom

The Outer Banks -> Raleigh, North Carolina

Not long ago, Michael drove out to Steve's cabin on the Outer Banks of North Carolina. Michael's son had just started an internship in the Bay Area and needed his car out there. The plan was simple: they would drive the car together to San Francisco, and Steve would fly home.

Michael had come in from Virginia for what was supposed to be a straightforward trip. But the moment he stepped inside the cabin, Steve could tell something heavier was riding along with him.

That evening, they sat on the back deck overlooking the water, the sound of the ocean rolling in steadily beneath the fading light. A couple of cocktails rested on the railing between them as gulls circled lazily overhead.

After a few minutes of silence, Michael finally spoke.

"My son just started an internship in San Francisco," he said quietly. "I need to get his car out to him... but Steve"—he hesitated—"I don't know how I'm going to afford the rest of his college...or retire in my lifetime."

The words landed with a dull weight.

A father doing everything right—working hard, providing, sacrificing—yet still unable to break the tension between responsibility and reality.

Steve nodded slowly without judgment.

They talked a bit longer about family, about the trip ahead, and about life in general. Eventually, the conversation drifted—naturally—toward money.

The next morning, as the sun rose over the water, they loaded their bags into Michael's son's car and pulled away from the Outer Banks. The first stretch was slow—two-lane roads winding past sand dunes, fishing shacks, and quiet beach towns where life moves at its own gentle pace.

Steve had decided to take the driver's seat to give Michael a chance to let his mind breath and decompress a bit.

Michael stared out the window.

"It's funny," he said. "Everything feels so calm out here... but my head is anything but."

"That's exactly how most people live," Steve said. "Externally calm. Internally stressed."

As the miles passed, the road widened. Two lanes became four. The speed picked up. Fewer stoplights. More distance covered with each mile.

"You ever notice," Michael said, "how the ocean makes you feel small, but somehow... hopeful?"

"That's the beauty of it," Steve said. "It reminds you how big life can be—if you stop living inside the box someone else built for you."

Michael exhaled. "I feel like all my financial decisions have boxed me in."

"That's not an insult," Steve said kindly. "It's just an observation.

Your current financial position is the result of the decisions you've made over the years.

The good news? That means you can make new ones."

As the road opened fully into the interstate and traffic began to move faster, Steve glanced over at him.

"This is how real change starts," Steve said. "From here on... everything changes."

They merged fully onto the interstate, the horizon stretching wide ahead of them.

"Let me guess what you were taught about money," Steve said.

Michael smirked. "Probably the same as everyone else: work hard, save into a 401(k), maybe invest extra in the stock market when you can."

"Exactly," Steve said. "And listen—that's not terrible advice. But it's slow. Painfully slow. If everything goes perfectly, you might achieve financial freedom in 40 years."

"Forty years..." Michael muttered. "That's... discouraging."

"It is," Steve said. "But here's the real problem:

Most people were never prepared to be financially successful in the first place."

"How do you mean?"

"School doesn't teach it," Steve said. "Most parents couldn't teach it. Traditional investment strategies don't teach it. The result is simple:

Most people aren't programmed to succeed with money."

Michael frowned. "Programmed?"

"Yes," Steve said. "Your mind believes whatever it heard growing up. If you were told, 'Rich people are jerks,' then your brain subconsciously works to keep you from becoming one of those 'jerks'—even though that belief is completely inaccurate."

Michael stared at the road, absorbing it.

"So my mind has been pushing me away from the very thing I've been trying to reach?"

"Exactly," Steve said. "And that's why 'mindset' must change before your financial position can."

As the coastal plains widened around them, Steve continued.

"Let me show you how powerful 'mindset' really is. Studies show that 80% of lottery winners go bankrupt within five years."

Michael nearly choked. "Eighty percent? That can't be right."

"It's absolutely right," Steve said. "And many NFL and NBA players—guys making millions—end up bankrupt within a few years after retiring."

"How does that happen?" Michael asked quietly.

"Because they got more money...but kept the same mindset," Steve said. "If you don't update the inner programming, the outer results eventually return to their original state—a financial struggle."

The car fell silent except for the hum of the tires.

"So where does that put my mindset?" Michael asked. "Between the lottery winners...and who?"

"And Grant Cardone," Steve said.

Michael laughed. "Okay, now I'm interested."

"A few years ago," Steve said, "Discovery Channel challenged Grant Cardone. People claimed he built wealth because he already had money. So they stripped him of everything. New identity. No contacts. No money. No phone. Dropped him in a random town with $100."

"What happened?"

"In 90 days, he turned that $100 into more than $5 million."

Michael shook his head. "That's unreal."

"No," Steve said softly. "That's 'mindset'. And the goal on this trip is to keep pulling you closer to that side of the spectrum...instead of the lottery-winner mindset that could turn $5 million into $100." He smiled. "That's a talent too."

They continued west, fields and forests rolling past in soft patterns.

"So what does financial freedom actually mean?" Michael asked.

"Well," Steve said, "most people think of beaches or golf courses. But that's just marketing. Financial freedom looks different for everyone."

"For you?"

"For me and my wife?" Steve said. "Travel, culture, adventure, great food. But that's lifestyle.

The financial definition is simple:

Financial freedom is having enough passive cash flow to cover your expenses for life."

Michael nodded slowly. "That's... surprisingly clear."

"It is," Steve said. "But people complicate it with a 'magic number'—some giant pile of money they hope not to outlive."

Steve shook his head. "I spent ten years as a financial planner using that exact approach. Then I realized the flaw:

It only works if you retire on schedule...and die on schedule."

Michael burst out laughing. "That's not comforting."

"No, it isn't," Steve said. "Which is why we need better paths."

"There are two main approaches," Steve continued.

"The first is the Dave Ramsey path: cut everything, sacrifice everything, save every dollar."

Michael nodded. "I know that one."

"It works," Steve said. "But it's misery for most people."

"And the second?"

"The lifestyle-first path," Steve said. "That's the one I chose. I wanted to work from anywhere, travel whenever I wanted, and still earn great money. So I built businesses that could run from a laptop."

"You're basically a digital nomad," Michael said.

"In many ways," Steve said.

Michael smiled. "That sounds like freedom."

"It is," Steve said. "And here's my philosophy:

If I can reach financial independence fast but hate the journey...or reach it a little slower but love the experience...I choose love every time."

Michael nodded. "Me too."

As the interstate stretched wide ahead of them, Michael took a deep breath.

"You know...I've felt stuck for a long time," he said. "But now? It finally feels like I'm moving in the right direction."

"You are," Steve said.

"And by the time we reach San Francisco...you'll know how to stay on it for life."

MIKE'S WEALTH JOURNAL — Checkpoint One Reflections

- My financial situation is the result of my decisions — and that means I can change it.

- Traditional investing is the slow lane; I want a faster, smarter path.

- Most people aren't programmed to succeed financially, but that programming can be rewritten.

- Money without the right financial mindset disappears; the right financial mindset without money can still create millions.

- Financial freedom = passive income covering expenses for life.

- I can choose a journey I enjoy instead of one built on sacrifice.

- This road trip isn't about getting rich quick — it's about getting rich intentionally.

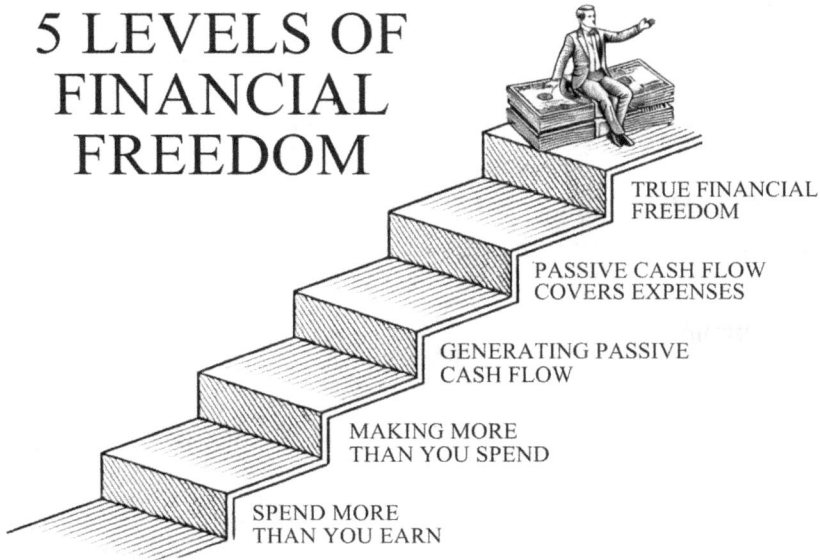

5 LEVELS OF FINANCIAL FREEDOM

TRUE FINANCIAL FREEDOM

PASSIVE CASH FLOW COVERS EXPENSES

GENERATING PASSIVE CASH FLOW

MAKING MORE THAN YOU SPEND

SPEND MORE THAN YOU EARN

CHAPTER 2:

UNDERSTAND YOUR STARTING POINT

Raleigh, North Carolina → Central North Carolina (I-40 West)

After Raleigh disappeared in the rearview mirror, the road settled into a steady rhythm. The traffic thinned. The skyline faded. Trees and open land replaced concrete and glass.

Michael watched the horizon for a long moment before breaking the silence.

"So this is really it," he said. "The start of the long road."

"It is," Steve replied. "And now that we're moving, it's time you understood exactly where you are on the mountain."

"The mountain?"

Steve smiled. "The five levels of financial freedom."

Michael leaned back. "All right. Walk me through it."

Steve kept his eyes on the road. "Level 1 is the furthest you can possibly be from financial freedom. At this level, you're spending more every month than you're making."

Michael exhaled. "That was me not long ago."

"If you're in Level 1," Steve said, "you need to get out — fast. Because this isn't the base of the mountain. It's not even the flatlands before the climb."

The land beside the highway dipped low in places, marshy and sunken.

"Think of the five levels like climbing a mountain," Steve continued. "The peak is your destination. Most people think Level 1 is the first slope of the mountain. It's not. Level 1 is miles away from the mountain — where the land drops to sea level. Some people are at sea level. Some are below it. Some are drowning far beneath the surface."

Michael nodded slowly. "That's exactly what it feels like."

"About 40% of Americans are right there with you," Steve said. "They spend more than they make. And listen — spending money is fun, it's easy, and it's necessary just to live. Food, shelter, clothes, gas. But earning enough is hard. That's why so many people get stuck here."

The road stretched flat and wide ahead of them.

After a few miles, the land began to firm up. The dips disappeared. The road felt more solid.

"Level 2," Steve said, "is where your income finally exceeds your expenses. You're no longer spending more than you make."

Michael's voice lifted. "That sounds like relief."

"It is," Steve said. "It's a massive improvement. You're no longer drowning. You can finally see the slopes of the mountain. You can actually start planning your climb."

"So what matters most at Level 2?" Michael asked.

"Priorities," Steve said. "Two of them. First — you take that extra money and attack high-interest debt. Credit cards. Anything bleeding you dry from Level 1."

"Clean up the damage," Michael said.

"Exactly. Second — you start building emergency savings and you begin investing for your future financial freedom. When your savings and investments start growing, your whole financial life becomes more stable."

Michael stared out at the passing fields. "Level 2 is solid ground."

"And solid ground is where real climbing begins," Steve said.

The road started to rise gently now. Not steep — but noticeable.

"Level 3," Steve said, "is where your investments begin generating passive cash flow."

Michael perked up. "So now the money is actually working."

"Now the money is officially on your team," Steve said. "You make more than you spend. The extra goes into investments. The investments start producing income. And that income goes right back into the investments."

"Compounding," Michael said.

"And compounding fast," Steve replied. "The numbers may start small — but small numbers that compound become big numbers quickly."

He glanced over. "Here's the key: the cash flow matters more than anything. You still work to make money — but now your money also works to make money."

Michael smiled. "It finally stops being a one-person effort. My investments work like a team that contributes to the effort."

The landscape began to feel different. The highway lifted just enough that the horizon shifted.

"Level 4," Steve said, "is where things get surreal."

Michael waited.

"You now have enough passive cash flow from your investments to cover your entire monthly expense budget."

Michael sat quietly.

"That doesn't mean you quit working forever," Steve continued. "But it means you could. If you got fired. If you quit. If you wanted to take time off. Your life no longer collapses if your job disappears."

Michael swallowed. "That changes everything."

"It does," Steve said softly. "You stop worrying about next month's bills. You stop panicking about emergencies. The most common cause of stress — financial stress — disappears. Most marriage fights are about money and those fade away. Your hobbies, your passions, your interests stop being limited by your budget."

"So money can't buy happiness..." Michael started.

"But it can absolutely reduce stress and pay for the activities that bring more joy into your life," Steve finished.

Michael nodded slowly. "And that's still not the top?"

Steve smiled. "No. That's just Level 4."

The road ahead rolled steadily upward now, stronger and more confident.

"Level 5," Steve said, "is when you have enough passive cash flow that you never need to work again."

Michael turned fully toward him. "That's the dream."

"The difference between Level 4 and Level 5," Steve explained, "is duration. On Level 4, your passive income might only last a short time — a few years, maybe longer. Not all cash flow is permanent."

"And Level 5?"

"Level 5 means the cash flow lasts as long as you do. Some investments pay for a few years. Some pay forever. When your expenses are covered by cash flow that lasts forever —and it increases with inflation- that's true financial freedom."

Michael sat in silence.

After a long stretch of highway, Michael finally spoke.

"So how do you move between them?"

Steve nodded. "That's the most important question of all. And the answer is different for everyone. Moving from Level 1 to Level 2 requires completely different actions than moving from Level 3 to Level 4. Even two people on the same level may need different strategies."

"So there's no single formula?"

"Yes. But before we get to that, I want to share some common paths," Steve said. "Keep in mind that everyone's exact route will always be personal."

He gestured ahead at the open road. "That's why we're out here right now — to give you the tools, the clarity, and the momentum to move up these levels as fast as possible."

Michael leaned back as trees rolled past in endless waves.

"For the first time," he said quietly, "I know exactly where I am."

Steve nodded. "And once you know that, the rest becomes possible."

MIKE'S WEALTH JOURNAL — Checkpoint Two Reflections

- Level 1 isn't just broke — it's drowning.

- Level 2 is solid ground and stability.

- Level 3 is when money begins to work for me.

- Level 4 removes stress, fear, and limitation.

- Level 5 means I never have to work again.

- About 40% of people live in Level 1 — I don't have to.

- Cash flow matters more than a giant pile of money.

- Every level requires different actions.

- I finally understand the mountain I'm climbing.

CHAPTER 3:

GET YOUR HEAD ABOVE WATER

Central North Carolina → Western North Carolina Foothills (I-40 West)

The land began to change as they continued west. The road was still wide and smooth, but the earth no longer felt flat. Gentle rises and dips rolled beneath the tires like the slow breathing of the land.

Michael stared ahead.

"So this is Level 1 in real life," he said. "The drowning level."

Steve nodded. "This is where most people spend their entire financial lives without ever realizing where they actually are."

Michael was quiet for a moment.

"Tell me about the people you've seen here."

Steve exhaled slowly.

"I've seen hundreds."

"First," Steve said, "let's talk about why people get stuck here. Because it's not just one reason. It's a pile-up of forces that work together."

Michael leaned in.

"Companies spend billions of dollars every year just to persuade you to buy their products," Steve said. "And they're better at selling than most people are at saying no."

Michael laughed. "That's true."

"Most people are hit with hundreds—if not thousands—of ads every single day. On their phone. Their TV. Their email. Their car. Their social feeds. Eventually, the mind gets worn down."

"Not only that, but spending money today is effortless," Steve continued. "Cash. Card. Phone. App. Tap. Swipe. One click. Businesses remove friction on purpose."

"And income still takes real effort," Michael said.

"Exactly," Steve replied. "Easy outflow. Hard inflow."

Steve smiled. "Let's be honest—spending money is fun. New clothes. Nice meals. Trips. Entertainment. You're not paying for the product— you're paying for how it makes you feel."

Michael nodded. "That hits home."

Steve's tone sharpened.

"They don't sell you a $49,000 car anymore. They sell you $599 monthly payment. Buy Now, Pay Later. Low monthly payments. So it feels affordable."

"And then the bills stack up," Michael said.

"And the moment an unexpected expense hits," Steve replied, "you realize you didn't budget for it—and you're stuck right back at Level 1."

Steve glanced over.

"Let me tell you about Bryan."

Michael turned fully toward him.

"Bryan was a sharp young guy. Great job. Around thirty years old. He came to me frustrated and said, 'Given what I earn, I think I should be in better financial shape than I am. What am I doing wrong?'"

Steve shook his head lightly.

"So I asked, 'Let's take a look at your budget.'"

Michael smiled. "Let me guess—he didn't have one."

Steve laughed. "The blank look on his face told me everything I needed to know. Bryan knew what he earned—but he had no idea what he was actually spending."

Michael leaned back slowly.

"That's a dangerous blind spot."

"It's one of the most common ones there is," Steve said.

"There are only two ways to climb from Level 1 to Level 2," Steve said.

Michael held up two fingers. "Expenses and income."

"Exactly."

"Reducing recurring expenses is the fastest lever," Steve said. "This means cutting what you already have—and being disciplined about not piling on more."

Michael smirked. "Like streaming services."

Steve laughed. "Exactly. Do you really need Netflix, Hulu, Apple TV, Paramount, and Prime?"

"And cars. And furniture. And toys," Michael added.

"Every recurring payment contributes to your drowning at Level 1," Steve said.

"The second route is increasing income," Steve said.

"Raises. Extra hours. A new job. A side hustle."

Michael nodded. "Ideally both, right?"

Steve smiled. "Exactly. Increase income and reduce expenses—and you accelerate your climb."

Steve continued, "Here's where most people sabotage themselves."

He paused.

"Let's say your expenses are $3,000 a month and your income is $3,000 a month. Then you get a raise and now you earn $4,000 a month."

Michael nodded. "Most people immediately upgrade their lifestyle."

"New car. New furniture. New payments," Steve said. "Their expenses jump right up to $4,000—and they're still broke."

"So what should happen?" Michael asked.

"Keep expenses at $3,000 and invest the extra $1,000," Steve said.

"That $1,000 becomes discretionary income—and that's the fuel for financial freedom."

Steve shook his head slowly.

"I've seen people making $50,000 a year who controlled their expenses and were closer to financial freedom than a doctor making $400,000 who spent everything."

Michael stared forward.

"That's... wild."

"It's not income that frees you," Steve said. "It's discipline."

Michael sighed.

"Every budget I've ever tried crashed and burned."

Steve smiled. "So did Bryan's. He told me, 'I tried years ago, but I couldn't predict exactly how much I'd spend on gas, food, and clothes—so I quit.'"

"That sounds familiar," Michael said.

"Two reasons most budgets fail," Steve said.

"First—people never finish them.

Second—when they do finish them, they're too complicated to follow."

"So what's the fix?" Michael asked.

Steve raised one finger.

"Keep it simple. Divide expenses into Essential and Fun."

Michael listened closely.

"Start with maybe 80% Essential and 20% Fun," Steve said. "Mortgage. Car. Insurance. Utilities are Essential. Dining out. Movies. Travel—that's Fun."

"Two bank accounts?" Michael asked.

Steve nodded. "Exactly. Paycheck comes in. Leave 80% in the main account. Transfer 20% to Fun. Only spend what's there."

"And no credit cards?" Michael said.

"Not until you're under control," Steve replied. "No Buy Now, Pay Later either."

"The more you automate," Steve added, "the easier finances become. Direct deposit. Automated transfers. Automated bill pay. Let technology do the discipline for you."

Michael smiled.

"That actually feels doable."

Steve's voice softened.

"One of the greatest traps at Level 1 is vanity."

"Keeping up with the Joneses," Michael said.

"Exactly," Steve replied. "The Joneses look rich—but they're buried in debt, stressed out, and fighting about money. Stop trying to keep up with that!"

Steve hesitated, then smiled.

"When my wife and I first got married, we each bought a new Mercedes."

Michael raised his eyebrows. "Nice."

"After five years?" Steve said. "All I had to show for it was a high payment and high maintenance bills. It slowed everything down."

"Later," Steve continued, "I bought a used Jeep. Drove it for almost ten years. No car payment for five of those years."

Michael nodded.

"When it was time to replace it, I could've bought another luxury car. Instead, I bought a Subaru. My payment is $361 a month while most of my neighbors pay over $1,000."

Michael smirked.

"That's a $650 monthly difference."

Steve nodded.

"And that difference changes investing, freedom, and lifestyle. Sure... driving a Mercedes felt nice, but driving a Subaru and having financial freedom feels much better."

Steve's voice grew firm.

"You will never achieve financial freedom if you stay on Level 1. Do whatever it takes to climb out."

Michael didn't speak for a long moment.

Then he finally said,

"I'm done drowning."

Steve smiled.

"Good. That's how the climb starts."

MIKE'S WEALTH JOURNAL — Checkpoint Three Reflections

- Level 1 traps people through ease, emotion, and advertising.

- Easy spending + easy credit is a dangerous mix.

- Income alone doesn't fix broken habits.

- Discretionary income is the fuel for freedom.

- A $50K disciplined life beats a $400K reckless one.

- Essential vs. Fun is the first budget that actually makes sense to me.

- Automation removes willpower from the process.

- Vanity is one of the most expensive mistakes people make.

- I don't need to look rich—I need to be free.

CHAPTER 4:

YOU THINK LIKE THE WEALTHY

Western North Carolina Foothills → Asheville, North Carolina (I-40 West)

The road narrowed slightly as the mountains began to assert themselves. Long, steady climbs replaced gentle hills. The engine worked harder now, and the scenery demanded attention.

Michael noticed it immediately.

"It feels different up here," he said. "Like the road is asking more of us."

Steve nodded. "That's a good way to put it. This is where most people stall — not because they can't go forward, but because they don't change how they think."

Michael glanced over. "You mean this is where Level 2 breaks down?"

"This is where Level 2 either turns into Level 3... or becomes a dead end."

Steve was quiet for a moment before speaking again.

"For years," he said, "I did everything the traditional investing world told me to do. I had a positive budget. I saved aggressively. I maxed out retirement accounts."

Michael nodded. "Sounds responsible."

"It was," Steve said. "Until it wasn't enough."

He tightened his grip on the steering wheel slightly.

"Unexpected expenses hit. More than one. My emergency fund wasn't enough to cover them."

Michael frowned. "Couldn't you tap your investments?"

"That was the problem," Steve said. "Most of my money was locked up. Retirement accounts. Long-term assets. On paper, I looked wealthy. In reality, I was stuck."

He glanced over.

"You've probably heard the phrase asset rich, but cash poor."

Michael nodded slowly. "That sounds... terrifying."

"It was," Steve said. "That moment put me in a very difficult position."

Steve took a breath.

"What came out of that moment was the biggest financial aha of my life."

Michael waited.

"I became obsessed with cash flow."

Steve continued, his voice steady now.

"I stopped focusing primarily on how much something was worth... and started focusing on how much money it produced every month."

Michael's eyebrows lifted.

"That single mindset shift," Steve said, "is what took me from a forty-year retirement path... to achieving financial freedom in five years."

Michael stared ahead.

Steve added quietly, "That is super important. Can you repeat what I just said?"

Michael smiled. "Uh-oh. A quiz. If I heard you correctly, you said that the mindset shift from asset values to focusing on cash flow first is what changed everything for you."

"Correct. You passed the test. The number one reason people can't move from Level 2 to Level 3," Steve said, "is that they never make this mental shift."

"Cash Flow First," Michael said.

"Exactly," Steve replied. "Society teaches us to chase appreciation. Buy and hold. Hope things go up."

He gestured vaguely. "Stocks. Hot tech companies. Crypto. Gold. Even some real estate."

"But none of that guarantees income," Michael said.

"Right," Steve said. "It only guarantees hope."

"You've probably seen the ads," Steve continued. "'What's your magic number?'"

Michael laughed. "All the time."

"I was a financial advisor for ten years," Steve said. "I know exactly how that number is calculated."

He paused.

"It works if your investments grow at the projected rate.

If your expenses grow at the projected rate.

If you withdraw the perfect amount.

If you don't live longer than expected."

Michael shook his head. "That's a lot of ifs."

"Too many," Steve said. "That's not a plan — that's a gamble."

Steve continued, "Let me ask you something."

Michael turned toward him.

"How often do you pay rent or a mortgage?"

"Monthly."

"Car payment?"

"Monthly."

"Utilities? Phone? Subscriptions?"

"Monthly," Michael said again.

Steve smiled. "Exactly. Life runs on monthly cash flow. It always has. And it always will."

He continued, "Financial freedom doesn't change that. A giant pile of money doesn't help unless it produces monthly income."

Steve leaned back slightly.

"Imagine you retire with a massive pile of gold coins," he said. "Every day, you remove some coins to pay for food, housing, life."

Michael nodded. "And you hope it lasts."

"You hope," Steve said. "And hoping is stressful."

He smiled slightly. "Now imagine you own a goose that lays a golden egg every single day."

Michael grinned. "Much better."

"You live off the eggs," Steve said. "You don't kill the goose. If you want more income, you get more geese."

"That's cash flow," Michael said.

"That's freedom," Steve replied.

Steve continued, "If my passive cash flow covers my expenses forever, do I care what the market value of those assets is?"

Michael thought for a moment. "No."

"Exactly."

"Let's say it's 2005," Steve said. "You own ten houses worth $100,000 each. Each one nets $750 a month in cash flow."

Michael did the math. "$7,500 a month in total cash flow."

"Right. Your portfolio is worth a million dollars. Then 2008 hits."

Michael nodded slowly.

"Values drop 50% almost overnight. Your portfolio loses half its value."

"So what do you do?" Michael asked.

"Nothing," Steve said calmly. "You keep collecting $7,500 a month."

Michael's eyes widened. "Because the cash flow never stopped."

"Exactly," Steve said. "The value didn't matter. The income did."

Steve's voice grew firm.

"That's how financial freedom is actually built. Not by chasing appreciation. By building passive cash flow."

Michael nodded slowly.

"To move from Level 2 to Level 3," Steve continued, "you must make this shift and start acquiring assets that produce income."

Michael exhaled deeply.

"I see it now," he said. "Level 2 gives you stability. Level 3 gives you momentum. But to move from Level 2 to 3, you must start acquiring assets that generate passive cash flow."

Steve smiled. "And that changes everything."

MIKE'S WEALTH JOURNAL — Checkpoint Four Reflections

- Being asset rich but cash poor is dangerous.

- Cash flow matters more than asset value.

- The biggest breakthroughs come from mindset shifts.

- The 'magic number' relies on too many assumptions.

- Life runs on monthly income — freedom should too.

- Hope is not a strategy.

- Passive cash flow creates resilience.

- Appreciation is optional; cash flow is essential.

- To reach Level 3, I must adopt a Cash Flow First mindset.

CHAPTER 5:

Your Money has Momentum

Great Smoky Mountains → Western Tennessee (I-40 West)

The climb became unmistakable now.

The road tightened. The trees closed in. Long stretches of uphill demanded steady pressure on the accelerator. Tractor-trailers slowed in the right lane while cars committed to the climb pressed forward.

Michael watched the incline carefully.

"It feels like we're finally gaining altitude," he said. "But it's work."

Steve nodded. "That's Level 3."

"Level 3," Steve said, "is when your investments start producing passive cash flow. Not someday. Not on paper. But real money — coming in every month."

Michael smiled. "That's when money finally stops being theoretical."

"Yes," Steve said. "And that's when people think they've arrived."

Michael glanced over. "But they haven't."

Steve smiled slightly. "Exactly."

Steve grew quiet for a moment as the mountains rolled past.

"There was a time many years ago that my wife hated her job," he said.

Michael turned fully toward him.

"It didn't start that way," Steve continued. "She's a pharmacist. She joined a small business early on. Everyone got along. The future looked bright."

He paused.

"Then the company grew fast. Too fast. Communication broke down. Workloads exploded."

Michael frowned. "Let me guess — long hours."

"Shifts scheduled to end at ten or eleven... that turned into two or three in the morning," Steve said. "Night after night."

He tightened his grip on the wheel.

"And this was while we were raising kids."

"At the time," Steve said, "we were asset rich... but cash flow poor."

Michael nodded slowly.

"She was exhausted. Stressed. Burned out," Steve said. "And there was nothing I could do."

"Why not?" Michael asked quietly.

"Because we hadn't built enough passive cash flow yet," Steve replied. "If we'd been on Level 4, I would've told her 'Honey, quit your job. We'll be fine.'— and she would've quit immediately."

Steve shook his head.

"But I couldn't say that. So she kept going. Not because she wanted to — but because she had no other option."

The car was silent for a long moment.

"The faster you reach Level 4," Steve said, "the faster situations like that become easy."

Michael nodded. "You quit. You breathe. You figure it out later."

"Exactly," Steve said. "Because your expenses are covered for a while. That's real freedom."

Michael broke the silence.

"So why don't more people make it from Level 3 to Level 4?"

Steve answered immediately.

"Discipline."

Michael leaned back. "They get comfortable."

"Yes," Steve said. "They see the cash flow coming in. They relax. They coast."

"And the climb stops."

Steve nodded. "They start spending more. Bigger vacations. Better cars. More entertainment."

He held up a hand. "I'm not saying don't enjoy life. I'm saying don't lose focus."

Steve continued, "Here's the simplest way I know to keep discipline."

Michael listened closely.

"You already have one account for Essential expenses. Hopefully one for Fun. Now you need a third — an Investment account."

Michael nodded. "Only for investing."

"Exactly," Steve said. "Because passive cash flow needs a destination."

"If passive cash flow goes into your Fun account," Steve said, "it dies."

Michael frowned. "It can't compound."

"It can't buy more assets. It can't accelerate your journey," Steve said. "But when it flows into an Investment account, it can cascade.."

Steve smiled. "Let's talk about cascading."

Michael raised an eyebrow.

"This is a hypothetical example to make the point, so ignore the returns for now. Assume you buy one asset for $12,000," Steve said. "It produces $1,000 a month of cash flow."

Michael did the math. "In twelve months, you've got $12,000 again."

"Right," Steve said. "Now you buy a second asset."

"Now you're making $2,000 a month."

"And in six months," Steve continued, "you've got enough to invest in a third asset."

Michael smiled. "$3,000 a month."

"And in four months," Steve said, "you're ready for a fourth."

"$4,000 a month," Michael said quietly.

Steve nodded. "That's the cascade. Cash flow from one asset cascades into two assets. Cash flow from two assets cascades into three assets... and so on."

"When you reinvest instead of spending," Steve said, "cash flow snowballs fast."

Michael stared ahead. "That's momentum."

"That's acceleration," Steve replied.

"This isn't theory," Steve said. "It's exactly what I did."

Michael turned to him.

"I started with just a few strong cash-flowing assets," Steve said. "I reinvested relentlessly."

He smiled.

"In three years, I turned three income sources into more than twenty."

Michael shook his head. "That's incredible."

Steve shrugged. "It was discipline."

Steve's voice was calm now. Certain.

"To move from Level 3 to Level 4, you only need three things."

Michael waited.

"Good investments. Discipline. Time."

The road ahead curved upward into Tennessee, steady and strong.

Michael nodded slowly.

"I see it now. Level 3 gives you hope... but discipline determines whether hope turns into freedom."

Steve smiled.

"And now you know why we don't take our foot off the gas."

MIKE'S WEALTH JOURNAL — Checkpoint Five Reflections

- Passive cash flow changes options — not just numbers.

- Being asset rich but cash-flow poor is a trap.

- Level 4 would have allowed freedom in moments of crisis.

- Level 3 tempts people to coast — discipline prevents that.

- Separate accounts protect momentum.

- Cash flow must be reinvested to compound.

- Cascading assets accelerate quickly when discipline is applied.

- Reinvestment turns years into months.

- Good investments + discipline + time = Level 4.

CHAPTER 6:

You Have Financial Peace of Mind

Tennessee Mountains → Central Tennessee (I-40 West)

The mountains softened as the road pushed deeper into Tennessee. The sharp climbs gave way to longer, steadier stretches. The engine no longer strained, but the road still demanded attention.

Michael noticed the shift.

"It feels... calmer," he said. "Like we've made it through the hardest part."

Steve nodded. "That's exactly how Level 4 feels."

Michael glanced over. "And that's what makes it dangerous?"

Steve smiled. "You're learning."

"Let me tell you about Charles and Barbara," Steve said.

Michael settled back into his seat.

"They came into my office in 2002, back when I was still a financial planner. They had done everything right. Worked hard. Saved for decades."

Steve paused.

"They were sixty-four. Charles had already picked his retirement date — about six months away."

Michael nodded. "They were ready."

"They thought they were," Steve said quietly.

Steve continued.

"They told me, 'Steve, three years ago we had about $700,000 ready for retirement. Last year, thanks to some tech stocks our advisor recommended, that grew to over a million dollars.'"

Michael raised his eyebrows.

"But then the dot-com bubble burst," Steve said. "Their account dropped to under $500,000."

Michael exhaled sharply. "Right before retirement."

"They looked at me and asked, 'What can you do to help us get back over a million so we can still retire this year?'"

Steve shook his head slowly.

"They thought they were on Level 5 — complete financial independence — only to have the rug pulled out from under them."

Michael waited.

"The only honest answer I could give them," Steve said, "was that they had three options."

He held up three fingers.

"Work longer. Slash their expenses. Or hope for an incredible market recovery."

Michael's jaw tightened.

"Do you know how it feels," Steve said quietly, "to tell someone that the plan they followed for forty years isn't going to work?"

Michael shook his head.

"To tell them they couldn't stop working. That they couldn't spend more time with their grandchildren."

The car fell silent.

After a few miles, Steve spoke again.

"Most people would say Charles and Barbara were diversified."

Michael frowned. "Weren't they?"

"They owned tech stocks, healthcare stocks, utilities, international funds," Steve said. "Sounds diverse, right?"

Michael nodded.

"The problem," Steve continued, "is that they were all stocks. And most stocks rise and fall together."

"So diversification wasn't real," Michael said.

"Exactly," Steve replied. "True diversification means owning assets that are not related to each other."

"You've heard the phrase 'don't put all your eggs in one basket,'" Steve said. "But most people just use different eggs... in the same basket."

Michael smiled. "So when the basket drops, everything breaks."

Steve nodded. "True diversification means different baskets entirely."

"Think back to 2022," Steve said. "Inflation jumped to nearly ten percent."

Michael nodded. "And the stock market dropped hard."

"Twenty to thirty percent," Steve said. "Now think about grocery prices."

"They skyrocketed," Michael said.

"One of the markets we invest in is agriculture," Steve explained. "Those investments earn cash flow based on harvest volume and market prices."

"So when food prices went up..." Michael started.

"The cash flow went up," Steve finished. "Stock market performance had zero impact on those investments."

Michael nodded slowly. "That's true diversification."

"To protect against market collapses," Steve said, "we emphasize diversification across multiple markets."

He counted them off.

"Stocks. Agriculture. Real estate. Business ownership. Secured lending. Digital assets like crypto."

Michael raised an eyebrow.

"It's not an all-inclusive list," Steve said, "but it provides diversification, strong returns, and passive cash flow."

"What about gold?" Michael asked.

"Precious metals. Collectibles. Fine art," Steve replied. "There are many others. They can all be part of a diverse portfolio, but the six I mentioned can provide cash flow."

Steve continued, "Another critical factor between Level 4 and Level 5 is time."

Michael leaned in.

"Not all cash-flowing assets last the same amount of time," Steve said. "So we group them into three categories."

"The first are called Infinite Assets because they generate cash flow forever," Steve said. "Real estate is a prime example. Maintain the property and it pays rent for life."

"Dividend stocks?" Michael asked.

"Exactly," Steve said. "You live on the dividends instead of selling the stock."

"The second category is Long Term. These produce income for decades — but not forever," Steve said. "Agriculture investments that last twenty-five to forty years. Promissory notes tied to mortgages that last thirty years."

Michael nodded. "Great income — but time-limited."

"Exactly," Steve said.

"The third category we call Short Term. These generate income for a short or unknown period," Steve said. "Often higher cash flow — but shorter lifespan."

Michael smiled. "Useful, but temporary."

Michael asked, "Why not just buy infinite assets from the beginning?"

Steve smiled. "Cost."

He continued, "If you need $3,000 a month and dividend stocks pay six percent, you need $600,000 invested."

"And real estate?" Michael asked.

"Four to five hundred thousand," Steve said. "That takes time."

"But there are short-term assets that could provide $3,000 a month with an initial investment as little as $30,000 to $100,000."

Steve smiled.

"Think of building a campfire. You don't start with giant logs."

"Paper first," Michael said.

"Exactly," Steve replied. "Fast-burning paper lights the twigs. The twigs light the long-burning logs."

"So short-term assets..." Michael began.

"...ignite long-term assets," Steve finished. "Which ignite infinite assets."

"Exactly! At Level 4," Steve said, "you already have enough passive cash flow to cover your monthly expenses for a while. At Level 5, you have enough passive cash flow to cover your expenses forever."

Michael nodded.

"Until then," Steve continued, "reinvest your passive cash flow into long-term and infinite assets."

"And if you have an emergency?" Michael asked.

"You stop reinvesting temporarily," Steve said. "Use the cash flow. Breathe. Then resume."

Steve's voice was steady.

"To move from Level 4 to Level 5, you need two things."

Michael waited.

"Understand how long your assets pay — and have the discipline to keep reinvesting."

The road ahead stretched west, wide and calm.

Michael exhaled slowly.

"So Level 5 isn't luck."

Steve smiled.

"It's structure."

MIKE'S WEALTH JOURNAL — Checkpoint Six Reflections

- Doing everything 'right' doesn't guarantee freedom.

- Market crashes expose weak plans.

- True diversification means non-correlated assets.

- Cash flow can rise when markets fall.

- Asset lifespan matters as much as yield.

- Infinite assets are the goal — not the starting point.

- Short-term assets ignite long-term growth.

- Reinvestment is what turns Level 4 into Level 5.

- Discipline and time complete the journey.

CHAPTER 7:

YOU HAVE ACHIEVED TRUE FINANCIAL FREEDOM

Central Tennessee → Western Tennessee (I-40 West)

The road smoothed out as they continued west. The steep climbs were behind them now, replaced by long, confident stretches of highway. The engine hummed steadily. The landscape felt open.

Michael noticed the change immediately.

"It doesn't feel like we're climbing anymore," he said. "It feels like we've... arrived."

Steve smiled. "That's Level 5."

Michael leaned back. "So this is what true financial freedom looks like."

"Yes," Steve said. "And it probably doesn't look the way most people imagine."

"Let me tell you about my friend Richard," Steve said.

Michael turned toward him.

"Richard is the clearest example I know of what Level 5 actually looks like," Steve continued. "Over the years, he built a collection of assets. They're diverse. They generate strong passive cash flow. A lot of them are in real estate, so the income is expected to last for decades."

Michael nodded. "So what does he do with all that freedom?"

Steve smiled. "He lives."

"He and his wife travel together," Steve said. "Richard loves fast cars. He owns a few. He races a few."

Michael laughed. "That sounds fun."

"It is," Steve said. "But here's the key — he didn't suffer for thirty or forty years to get there. He enjoyed the journey."

"So no burnout," Michael said.

"No burnout," Steve replied. "And no reckless spending either. He still lives responsibly."

Steve continued, "Remember the goose that lays golden eggs?"

Michael smiled. "Hard to forget."

"Richard acquired several geese over the years," Steve said. "And he has the discipline to live within the budget those eggs provide."

Michael nodded. "He doesn't kill the goose."

"That's financial freedom," Steve said. "Stress-free. Intentional. Enjoyable."

"One thing people misunderstand," Steve added, "is that financial freedom doesn't mean you must stop working."

Michael raised an eyebrow.

"Richard was a real estate agent...and still is." Steve said. "So he still represents buyers and sellers from time to time. But now it's because he wants to — not because he has to."

Michael nodded slowly. "That's a big difference."

"I also know people," Steve continued, "who could quit their primary job — but don't want to."

Michael thought for a moment. "So what happens when both their job and their investments cover their expenses?"

Steve smiled. "They have options."

"There are three main things people do with excess cash flow," Steve said.

Michael listened.

"One — they spend more. They enjoy the life they've built."

"That makes sense," Michael said.

"Two — they keep acquiring assets and increase their passive cash flow even further."

"And the third?" Michael asked.

"Emergency assets," Steve replied.

Steve continued, "I like to think of assets as streams and wells."

Michael smiled. "Okay, explain."

"Imagine living in the woods ten thousand years ago," Steve said. "You live by a stream that provides all the water you need."

Michael nodded.

"If the stream produces more water than you need," Steve continued, "you could store some in a well."

"So the stream keeps flowing," Michael said, "and the well is backup."

"Exactly," Steve said.

"A stream," Steve explained, "is an asset that produces ongoing passive cash flow. Rental income is a perfect example."

"And a well?" Michael asked.

"Emergency assets that may still grow — like gold, ETFs, or other non-cash-flow assets," Steve said. "They're there if you need extra water."

Steve smiled softly.

"A friend of mine recently cashed in an old mutual fund," he said. "He used it to take his two kids, their spouses, and his five grandkids to Disney."

Michael's eyes lit up. "That's incredible."

"It's an experience they'll remember forever," Steve said. "That's what financial freedom makes possible."

"One more thing about Richard," Steve added. "He still learns."

Michael nodded.

"He still reads about investing. He still reviews his portfolio. He still makes adjustments."

Steve smiled. "And that's where the mountain analogy breaks down."

"When you climb a mountain," Steve said, "you reach the peak, celebrate, take pictures, and head back down."

Michael smiled. "But Level 5 isn't like that."

"No," Steve said. "When you reach Level 5, you don't stop."

He paused.

"Never stop learning.

Never stop monitoring.

Never stop adjusting."

The road stretched west, open and endless.

Michael exhaled slowly.

"So Level 5 isn't the end."

Steve smiled.

"It's the beginning — on your terms."

MIKE'S WEALTH JOURNAL — Checkpoint 7 Reflections

True financial freedom is cash flow that lasts for life.

Freedom is about choice, not excess.

Discipline protects the golden goose.

Working becomes optional — not mandatory.

Excess cash flow creates options, not pressure.

Streams provide income; wells provide security.

Wealth creates memories, not just numbers.

Learning never stops at Level 5.

Financial freedom is a journey — not a finish line.

THE SECRET FORMULA FOR WEALTH CREATION

CHAPTER 8:

THE EXPONENTIAL WEALTH FORMULA

Western Tennessee → Crossing the Mississippi River (I-40 West)

The land flattened as they pushed west. The hills softened. The road straightened. Ahead, the Mississippi River waited — wide, powerful, and impossible to ignore.

Michael watched the horizon.

"This part of the drive feels different," he said. "Like we've crossed into something bigger."

Steve nodded. "We have."

Michael glanced over. "So this is where the formula comes in."

Steve smiled. "This is where wealth stops growing linearly... and starts multiplying."

"Let me tell you about Howard Schultz," Steve said.

Michael nodded. "Starbucks."

"Yes," Steve replied. "But most people don't know how that story really started."

"Schultz grew up in public housing in Brooklyn," Steve said. "First in his family to graduate college. He went to Northern Michigan University on a football scholarship."

Michael raised his eyebrows. "That's not exactly Silicon Valley."

"No," Steve said. "His father was a blue-collar worker. No benefits. No safety net. Watching that struggle shaped him."

"Later," Steve continued, "Schultz joined Starbucks as the director of retail operations and marketing. Back then, Starbucks just sold coffee beans."

Michael frowned. "No cafés?"

"None," Steve said. "Then in 1983, Schultz traveled to Milan."

Michael smiled. "Let me guess — coffee bars."

"Exactly," Steve said. "He saw community. Connection. Conversation. He believed Starbucks could be more than a product — it could be a place."

"But the founders didn't agree," Steve continued. "They rejected his vision."

Michael leaned forward. "So what did he do?"

"He left," Steve said. "In 1985, he started his own company — Il Giornale."

Michael whistled. "Risky."

"Very," Steve said. "He was rejected 217 times by investors before finally securing funding."

Michael shook his head. "Most people quit after ten."

"In 1987," Steve said, "the original Starbucks founders decided to sell."

Michael's eyes widened. "And Schultz was ready."

"He raised the money, bought Starbucks, and rebuilt it according to his vision."

Steve continued, "He focused on customer experience. He gave employees healthcare, stock ownership, even free college tuition."

Michael nodded slowly. "He invested in people."

"Under Schultz's leadership," Steve said, "Starbucks grew from 11 stores to over 28,000 locations in 77 countries."

Michael exhaled. "That's insane."

"Today," Steve added, "Starbucks employs roughly 300,000 to 400,000 people."

"With that example, can you tell me how he created his wealth?"

Michael paused.

"By starting a business?"

Steve smiled. "Sort of."

Steve continued, "He used the most important resources on earth."

Michael waited.

"Time. Money. Knowledge."

"You can't create wealth if you spend zero minutes on it...time is required" Steve said. "And you've heard the phrase 'it takes money to make money.' That's often true. And, you must have the knowledge of what to do."

Michael nodded.

"But there are two keys that most people miss," Steve said. "First of all, these three parts of the formula don't add."

He paused.

"They multiply."

Michael sat up straighter.

"A big increase in one helps," Steve continued. "But a small increase in all three is even more powerful."

Steve emphasized it.

"Every improvement in any one area amplifies the entire result."

Michael repeated it quietly. "Every improvement multiplies."

"Let's test the formula," Steve said. "Remember the lottery winners?"

Michael nodded. "Millions... gone in five years."

"Let's rate their time, money, and knowledge on a scale of zero to five,"

Steve said. "Money: maybe a 4. Time: a 4 or 5 — they quit working."

"And knowledge?" Michael asked.

"Zero," Steve said.

Michael grimaced. "Four times four times zero..."

"...equals zero," Steve finished. "If they'd had even a little knowledge, their outcome would've been completely different."

"Now think about Grant Cardone," Steve continued.

Michael smiled. "The $100 reset."

"Exactly," Steve said. "Money: basically a 1. Time: a 5. Knowledge: a 5."

Michael did the math. "Twenty-five."

"And after 90 days," Steve added, "his money wasn't a 1 anymore."

Michael nodded. "Now the formula explodes."

"That's how people like Grant Cardone, Elon Musk, Warren Buffett, and Howard Schultz keep multiplying wealth," Steve said.

Michael leaned back. "They keep feeding the formula."

Steve glanced toward the Mississippi River as it came into view.

"Here's the part that changes everything," he said. "This is the part that most people never even consider."

Michael turned.

"The formula is Time x Money × Knowledge," Steve said. "But I never said it had to be your time, your money, or your knowledge."

Michael's eyes widened.

"That's the twist," Steve said. "Howard Schultz didn't scale Starbucks alone. He leveraged funding. Teams. Expertise."

"And now hundreds of thousands of people multiply the formula for him," Michael said quietly.

Steve smiled. "Exactly."

They crossed the Mississippi River as the sun reflected off the water.

Steve continued, "And starting next... I'll show you how to do the same."

MIKE'S WEALTH JOURNAL — Checkpoint 8 Reflections

- Wealth accelerates when resources multiply, not add.

- Time, money, and knowledge are the core levers.

- Every small improvement amplifies the result.

- Knowledge prevents collapse; ignorance multiplies loss.

- Scale comes from leveraging resources beyond your own.

- Exponential growth begins with understanding the formula.

- The journey just entered a new phase.

CHAPTER 9:

USE LEVERAGE TO ACCELERATE RESULTS

Eastern Arkansas → Arkansas Delta (I-40 West)

The Mississippi River was behind them now, but its presence still lingered.

The land flattened into wide, open stretches. Long fields. Quiet towns. The road felt steady, dependable — like it had been carrying commerce, trade, and movement for generations.

Michael broke the silence.

"So this is where leverage comes in."

Steve nodded. "This is where people finally realize they don't have to do everything alone."

"The goal of financial independence," Steve said, "is to build your wealth — your money. But here's the truth most people never hear."

Michael waited.

"It's often easier to build your wealth using somebody else's money."

Michael smiled. "OPM."

"Exactly," Steve said. "Other People's Money. And no — not the Danny DeVito movie."

Michael laughed. "Shame."

Steve glanced out at the flat land rolling by.

"Let me give you a real example," he said. "Years ago, I found a seller who owned his house free and clear. No mortgage."

"I asked him if I could pay for the house over time," Steve said. "He agreed. We settled on $804 a month for 60 months."

Michael did the math quietly. "About $40,000?"

"Yes. Then," Steve continued, "I found a tenant willing to rent the property for $800 a month."

Michael raised an eyebrow. "That's close."

"Very close," Steve said. "And I got lucky — that tenant stayed the full five years."

Steve continued, deliberately.

"For five years, I paid the seller $804 a month — using his money to buy the house."

Michael nodded.

"For five years, the tenant paid me $800 a month."

Michael smiled.

"I used the tenant's money — OPM — to pay the seller."

Michael leaned back.

"For five years, I lost four dollars a month."

Michael laughed. "That's almost nothing."

"And after five years," Steve said, "the house was paid off and I sold it for $75,000."

Michael sat up straight.

"My total out-of-pocket investment?" Steve continued. "$240 over five years."

Michael shook his head. "That's insane."

Steve smiled. "Given what I know now, I never would have sold it — but we'll get to that later."

Michael grew quiet.

"So when people say, 'It takes money to make money...'"

"They're only half right," Steve said. "Money helps — but it can be Other People's Money."

"There's no rule that says you must use your own," Michael said.

"Exactly," Steve replied.

"Real estate is one of the most common ways to use OPM," Steve said. "But it's not the only one."

Michael nodded.

"Remember Howard Schultz?" Steve asked.

"The Starbucks story," Michael said.

"He had the vision," Steve continued. "But he needed capital. Without OPM, Starbucks might still be eleven coffee shops in Seattle."

"You can use OPM in many other ways," Steve said.

Michael leaned in.

"Most brokerage accounts allow you to borrow up to 50% of your portfolio value. That's called margin."

Michael nodded. "Using stocks as collateral."

"Exactly," Steve said. "Some allow you to reinvest it. Others let you withdraw it as cash."

"More institutions are allowing crypto as collateral," Steve continued. "Chase Bank recently announced you could borrow against Bitcoin."

Michael raised his eyebrows. "Using OPM from a bank to invest elsewhere."

"Same with gold," Steve said. "There are institutions that will store gold for you and lend against it."

Michael exhaled. "So assets unlock leverage."

Steve's tone shifted slightly.

"Yes." he said, "Which leads to a talk about responsibility."

Michael nodded. "Because leverage cuts both ways."

"Exactly," Steve said.

"Did you notice something about every example I gave?" Steve asked.

Michael thought for a moment. "Every loan was backed by an asset."

"Yes," Steve said. "Real estate. Stocks. Gold. Crypto. There was always collateral."

"That's the difference between good debt and bad debt," Steve said.

Michael listened carefully.

"Good debt is used to acquire or grow an asset — something that appreciates and/or produces cash flow."

"And bad debt?" Michael asked.

"Debt used for liabilities," Steve said. "Things that lose value or produce nothing."

Steve continued, "If you borrow $20,000 for a car, you have payments — and the asset loses value."

Michael nodded. "Unless it produces income."

"Right," Steve said. "Driving for Uber would change the math."

"And credit cards?" Michael asked.

Steve shook his head. "The worst example. Movies, meals, vacations — those don't generate income or appreciation."

Michael smiled. "Even though they're fun."

"They're sunk costs," Steve said. "And I spend money on them too."

Michael asked, "So is there a limit?"

Steve smiled. "Apparently $25 billion is acceptable if your name is Elon Musk."

Michael laughed.

"But for the rest of us," Steve continued, "it's not about a dollar amount. It's about ratios."

"Real estate lenders typically loan 70–80% of a property's value," Steve said. "That protects them if prices drop."

Michael nodded.

"Stock margin is usually capped at 50% because stocks are volatile."

"And gold and crypto?" Michael asked.

"Similar formulas," Steve replied.

"Businesses are trickier," Steve said. "They can skyrocket in value — or drop to zero."

Michael frowned. "Unlike real estate or gold."

"Exactly," Steve said. "That's why lenders approach business loans very carefully."

Michael looked out across the wide Arkansas fields.

"So OPM isn't about recklessness," he said. "It's about structure."

Steve smiled. "And responsibility."

Michael nodded slowly.

"Used wisely... it accelerates everything."

Steve glanced ahead at the long stretch of highway.

"And now," he said, "you're ready for the next lever."

MIKE'S WEALTH JOURNAL — Checkpoint 9 Reflections

- Wealth doesn't require using only my own money.

- Leverage accelerates wealth when used responsibly.

- Every example of leverage included real collateral.

- Good debt builds assets; bad debt funds consumption.

- Ratios matter more than dollar amounts.

- OPM is a tool — not a shortcut.

CHAPTER 10:

HAVE OTHERS BUILD YOUR WEALTH

Eastern Oklahoma → Oklahoma City (I-40 West)

The road opened wide as they crossed into Oklahoma.

Long, uninterrupted stretches of highway. Big sky. Fewer exits. The kind of road that gave your thoughts room to breathe.

Michael leaned back in his seat.

"You know what's funny?" he said. "I used to think knowledge was optional once you had money."

Steve smiled. "That mistake has cost a lot of very rich people everything."

"Let me tell you a story," Steve said. "About a man who could've coasted for life."

Michael glanced over. "Is it someone I know?"

Steve nodded. "Shaquille O'Neal. Shaq was a beast on the basketball court. But what he did off the court may be more amazing."

Michael waited.

"While he was playing in the NBA," Steve said, "people constantly pitched him business and investment ideas. But they always talked to his agent — even when Shaq was sitting right there."

Michael frowned. "That would drive me crazy."

"It certainly drove him crazy," Steve said. "So he decided to do something about it."

"He went back to school," Steve continued. "Got his MBA through the University of Phoenix — in person."

Michael's eyebrows shot up. "While playing in the NBA?"

"Yes," Steve said. "And here's the best part: the minimum class size was sixteen. So Shaq paid for fifteen of his friends to get their MBA with him."

Michael laughed. "That's next-level commitment."

"That's understanding the value of knowledge," Steve said.

"Studies show that about 60% of NBA players are broke within five years of retirement," Steve said. "Same story as lottery winners — money without literacy."

Michael nodded. "Money dumped into their lap."

"Shaq was different," Steve said. "Because once he had knowledge, he knew how to spot good opportunities."

Steve ticked them off casually.

"Early investor in Ring — the doorbell camera."

Michael whistled.

"Over 150 Five Guys franchises."

"Wow."

"About 150 car washes.

Around 40 24-Hour Fitness centers.

Papa John's.

Started Big Chicken restaurants.

Owns real estate.

Owns nightclubs."

Michael shook his head. "That's not luck."

"No," Steve said. "That's knowledge meeting money."

"Shaq didn't just make money and spend it," Steve continued. "He followed advice to save 75% of his income."

Michael blinked. "Seventy-five?"

"Then," Steve said, "he gained the knowledge on how to invest it wisely."

Michael exhaled. "That's discipline and education."

"One of my favorite investing books," Steve said, "is The Richest Man in Babylon."

Michael nodded. "I have heard of it."

"There's a simple rule in it," Steve continued. "Never invest in something unless you are an expert in the investment— or you have a trusted advisor who is."

Michael smiled knowingly. "People ignore that all the time."

Steve chuckled softly.

"'Hey Steve, my brother-in-law made a fortune trading gold futures, so I tried.'

Not an expert. Didn't hire one. Lost the investment."

Michael winced.

"'Hey Steve, I saw a video about Forex — I'm starting tomorrow.'

Not an expert. Didn't hire one. Lost it all."

Michael shook his head.

"'Hey Steve, my friend recommended a meme coin.'

Not an expert. Didn't hire one. Lost 90%."

Michael sighed. "Same mistake. Different wrapper."

"Here's the breakthrough," Steve said. "Knowledge is part of the Exponential Formula."

Michael nodded.

"But," Steve continued, "you're not limited to your knowledge."

Michael smiled. "OPK."

"Exactly," Steve said. "Other People's Knowledge."

"One of my favorite quotes," Steve said, "is this:

'Wealth is created with concentration. Wealth is protected with diversification.'"

Michael repeated it quietly.

"People get rich by focusing deeply on one thing," Steve continued. "For me, it was real estate. For others, it's Forex, options, crypto, business, or their career."

Michael nodded. "Doctors. Lawyers. Engineers."

"Exactly," Steve said. "They concentrate to generate money— then diversify."

Steve paused for a moment.

"I used to think I could figure everything out myself," he said. "If I found an interesting investing opportunity, I'd read about it. Perhaps watch some videos. Then try it."

Michael smiled. "Sounds familiar."

"I had knowledge," Steve said. "But I wasn't an expert."

"When I first owned rental properties," Steve said, "I managed them myself."

Michael leaned in.

"One unit should've rented for $750. I listed it. Nothing. Dropped to $725. Nothing. $695. Nothing. Five months vacant."

Michael grimaced. "Ouch."

"Why?" Steve said. "So I could avoid paying a property manager 10%."

Michael laughed. "Classic."

"Finally, I hired one," Steve continued. "They rented it for $725 in two weeks because they had more knowledge on renting properties than I did."

Michael did the math. "Even after their fee..."

"My net was $652.50," Steve said. "I was about to drop it to $600 and do all the work myself. By handing it off to them, I made more money and never had to deal with tenants again."

Michael shook his head. "That's expensive pride."

"That's when I decided to 'play dumb,'" Steve said. "I stopped pretending to know everything."

Michael smiled. "And started hiring experts who already had the knowledge?"

"Yes," Steve said. "I asked better questions. Sought proof. Required results."

"I didn't take advice from anyone who said they were an expert," Steve continued. "I needed proof."

Michael chipped in "Lots of false claims."

"Yep. I refused to work with anyone who wasn't at least a millionaire," Steve said. "Too many so-called 'experts' make money selling advice — who never made money following their advice."

"One of my biggest breakthroughs," Steve said, "was joining a MasterMind group."

Michael looked intrigued.

"Top real estate investors from coast to coast," Steve said. "We met a few times a year. Each of us shared what worked best for us."

Michael smiled. "People with money talk about money."

"Exactly," Steve said. "That's how you grow."

Steve continued, "Every millionaire I know credits coaches, mentors, advisors."

Michael nodded. "Self-made millionaire is a myth."

"A terrible one," Steve said. "Build your team. I guarantee that if you interviewed 100 multi-millionaires, not one of them would say that they created their wealth all by themselves."

As Oklahoma City came into view, Michael spoke quietly.

"So knowledge isn't optional," he said. "It's leverage."

Steve smiled. "Always be building your knowledge...and using OPK because it multiplies everything."

MIKE'S WEALTH JOURNAL — Checkpoint 10 Reflections

- Money without knowledge disappears.

- Knowledge without experts is incomplete.

- OPK accelerates results dramatically.

- Concentration creates wealth; diversification protects it.

- Pride is expensive; experts are efficient.

- No one builds wealth alone.

- Teams multiply outcomes.

CHAPTER 11:

LEARN TO CREATE MORE TIME

Texas Panhandle → Amarillo, Texas (I-40 West)

The landscape flattened completely as they crossed deeper into Texas.

The road stretched straight to the horizon — mile after mile of sameness. No shortcuts. No detours. Just forward motion.

Michael broke the silence.

"You ever notice how time feels distorted on roads like this?"

Steve smiled. "That's because there's nowhere to hide from it."

"You ever seen Back to the Future?" Steve asked.

Michael laughed. "Of course."

"How many time travel movies can you name?" Steve continued. "Five? Ten? Twenty?"

Michael thought for a moment. "A lot."

"There are hundreds," Steve said. "I once Googled 'best time-travel movies' and was amazed at how many there are."

Michael nodded. "People love that idea."

"Because," Steve said, "we're all searching for a solution to the one thing we can't control."

"The sun keeps rising," Steve continued.

"The clocks keep ticking."

Michael stared at the road. "No pause button."

"No rewind," Steve said. "No extensions."

"So why," Michael asked, "is time part of the Exponential Wealth Formula if everyone gets the same amount?"

Steve smiled. "Great question. Because while you can't control time... you can control how you use it."

"There are two ways," Steve said, "to increase the impact of time on your wealth."

Michael nodded. "Let's hear them."

"First," Steve said, "how much time will you actually spend building your wealth?"

Michael frowned slightly.

"Most people," Steve continued, "spend more time planning a vacation than planning their financial future."

Michael exhaled. "That's painfully true."

"If wealth matters," Steve said, "it deserves time on your calendar."

"But here's the real unlock," Steve said. "You're not limited to your time."

Michael smiled. "OPT."

"Exactly," Steve said. "Other People's Time."

"If you know what you're doing," Steve said, "you can make great money trading crypto."

Michael nodded. "High skill. High focus."

"I could eventually figure it out," Steve said. "But then I'd need to spend hours every day managing it."

"So you didn't," Michael said.

"No," Steve replied. "I hired an expert."

"He runs a crypto trading fund," Steve said.

"He has the knowledge. He spends the time."

Michael asked, "How did it perform?"

Steve replied calmly, "At least 3% per month, every month, for its first 36 months."

Michael's eyebrows shot up. "That's serious."

"OPK and OPT working together," Steve said.

"Second," Steve continued, "delegate tasks that eat time."

Michael nodded.

"I own and manage eight businesses," Steve said. "Tracking transactions alone takes hours."

Michael laughed. "Accounting flashbacks?"

"I have the knowledge," Steve said. "But my time is better spent elsewhere."

"So you hired a bookkeeper."

"Exactly," Steve said. "They handle the details. I focus on growth."

Steve paused.

"Now this one," he said, "changes everything."

Michael leaned in.

"Instead of seeing OPT as an expense," Steve said, "you can get paid for it."

"Imagine you're a plumber," Steve said.

"You earn $50 per hour."

Michael nodded. "Only paid when you work."

"Work 40 hours," Steve continued, "you make $2,000. Take a week off — you make nothing."

Michael shrugged. "That's most people."

"Now," Steve said, "you hire four plumbers at $40 per hour."

Michael started doing the math.

"You charge clients $60 per hour," Steve continued.

"Every hour they work, you make $20."

Michael smiled. "And you're not holding the wrench."

"If all four are working," Steve said, "you make $80 per hour."

Michael nodded. "That's $3,200 per week."

"Even after paying a salesperson," Steve said, "you earn about what you did before."

"But here's the difference," Steve said.

Michael waited.

"When you go on vacation... you still earn $80 per hour."

"When you get sick... you still earn $80 per hour."

Michael leaned back. "That's freedom."

Steve continued, "That's why lawyers want to become partners."

Michael smiled. "Leverage."

"A young attorney might be paid $100 per hour," Steve said.

"But billed at $200–300 per hour."

Michael nodded. "The difference goes to the partners."

"Let's say a firm has 10 young attorneys," Steve said.

"They work 40 hours a week."

Michael followed closely.

"And the firm earns $150 per hour per attorney," Steve continued.

"That's $1,500 per hour... or $60,000 per week."

Michael whistled. "That covers rent."

"And then some," Steve said.

"The partners aren't billing hours," Steve said.

"They're leveraging OPT."

Michael stared ahead as Amarillo came into view.

"So time can't be controlled," he said slowly.

"But it can be multiplied."

Steve smiled. "Now you're thinking exponentially."

MIKE'S WEALTH JOURNAL — Checkpoint 11 Reflections

- Time never stops, but it can be used wisely.

- Planning wealth deserves scheduled time.

- OPT allows results without personal effort.

- Delegation increases returns and frees focus.

- Businesses scale by leveraging other people's hours.

- Wealth flows faster when time is multiplied.

STRATEGIES TO ACCELERATE YOUR JOURNEY

F

CHAPTER 12:

UNDERSTAND THE GREATEST WEALTH CREATOR
OF ALL TIME

Eastern New Mexico → Albuquerque, New Mexico (I-40 West)

Michael watched the landscape roll by for a few moments before speaking.

"You know," he said, "most people think investing is just putting money somewhere and waiting. Stocks. Bonds. Crypto. Gold. Maybe a private loan or two. You park your money and hope it grows."

Steve nodded. "That's how most people are taught to think about it."

"And don't get me wrong," Michael continued. "That kind of investing matters. But it feels...slow."

Steve smiled. "That's because it is."

Michael glanced over. "Meaning?"

"There's a difference between growing wealth and creating wealth," Steve said. "Most investments grow what you already have. Creation is different. Creation accelerates the process."

Michael thought about that.

"So you're saying financial freedom comes faster when you're not just waiting for appreciation."

"Exactly," Steve said. "If you want to compress time, you need leverage. And historically, there are two vehicles that have done that better than anything else."

Michael frowned slightly. "Okay... leverage."

He paused. "I'm drawing a blank."

Steve smiled. "That's alright. Most people do. Let's work backward. Think about the wealthiest people you know — not celebrities, just real people."

Michael shrugged. "They don't just earn salaries."

"Good," Steve said. "Keep going."

"They own... something," Michael said slowly. "Assets. Operations. Cash flow."

Steve nodded but said nothing.

Michael stared out the windshield for a moment. "Some of them own properties."

Steve raised an eyebrow.

"And some own companies," Michael added, almost testing the words.

He glanced over. "Real estate and business?"

Steve grinned. "Every time. Even a small business — especially one that's managed — can completely change someone's financial trajectory."

Michael looked back out at the road as the scenery began to shift.

The road began to change again.

The Texas flatlands faded behind them, replaced by wider skies, mesas in the distance, and a sense of space that made everything feel bigger — including possibility.

Michael looked out at the horizon.

"You know," he said, "it feels like this is where the road really opens up."

Steve nodded. "That's a good instinct. This is where wealth creation gets serious."

"Let me ask you something," Steve said. "If you looked at the thousand richest people in America, what do you think most of them have in common?"

Michael thought for a moment.

"Business owners?"

"Exactly," Steve said. "Most created their wealth by owning a business. The rest? Real estate."

Michael shrugged. "Most of the richest started some big tech company, so I suppose this is a new development."

Steve smiled. "It's ancient."

"Go back two hundred years," Steve continued. "Who were the wealthiest people?"

"Merchants and landlords," Michael said.

"Go back a thousand years. Two thousand. Same answer," Steve said. "The tools change, but the pattern doesn't."

Michael chuckled. "Except kings and emperors."

Steve laughed. "Well...I don't think I could help you become one of those."

"Whenever I say this," Steve continued, "someone usually responds with: 'I don't have the resources to own a business.'"

Michael nodded. "Time. Money. Knowledge."

"And remember," Steve said, "you can use OPM, OPK, and OPT."

"Have you ever heard of Madame C.J. Walker?" Steve asked.

Michael frowned. "I don't think so."

Steve nodded. "Most people haven't. And that's a shame."

"She was born in Louisiana in 1867," Steve said. "Two years after slavery ended. Her parents were formerly enslaved."

Michael's expression changed.

"She lost both parents and became an orphan," Steve continued. "No education. No money."

Michael shook his head. "And every systemic disadvantage imaginable."

"She was Black. She was a woman. Equality wasn't even a conversation yet," Steve said. "And here's the real kicker — she didn't have the internet."

Michael laughed softly. "No YouTube tutorials."

"No Google. No online investors. No Amazon storefront," Steve said. "Nothing."

"She suffered from hair loss," Steve said. "Instead of accepting it, she created hair and beauty products for Black women."

Michael nodded slowly.

"She trained thousands of sales agents," Steve continued. "Built an empire. Became the first self-made Black female millionaire in America."

Michael exhaled. "That puts things in perspective."

Steve looked at him.

"Your starting point is better than hers. What will you do with it?"

"Not only did she become very successful, but she gave back," Steve continued. "Left a legacy. She spent part of her later life in Indianapolis — where the Madame Walker Theatre opened in 1927."

Michael smiled. "That's impact."

"That's business ownership," Steve said.

"So how does it work?" Michael asked.

"Simple," Steve replied. "You provide something people want or need."

Michael nodded. "Like hair products."

"You sell it for more than it costs to provide," Steve said. "That's profit."

Michael smiled. "Like selling plumbing services for $100 an hour and paying plumbers $50."

"Exactly," Steve said. "That spread is where wealth is created."

"And here's what most people overlook," Steve continued. "A profitable business can be sold."

Michael raised an eyebrow.

"You build it. Enjoy the cash flow. Then sell it for a multiple of earnings," Steve said.

Michael nodded. "That's real wealth."

"And then there are the tax benefits," Steve added. "Lots of them."

Michael laughed. "I knew that was coming."

"The tax code was written by wealthy people who own businesses and real estate," Steve said. "Travel is one of my favorite activities."

"When I visited my coffee plantation investment in Panama," Steve said, "that was a business expense."

Michael smiled. "Nice."

"I have partners and ventures all over the U.S.," Steve continued. "I can visit almost anywhere, conduct some business, and deduct the travel."

"Most people think starting a business is complicated," Steve said.

Michael nodded. "Or expensive."

"You can start one for $100 in about ten minutes," Steve said.

Michael laughed. "That's dangerously easy."

"But," Steve added, "if you stop there, you make no money."

"You can approach business ownership the same way people own rental properties," Steve said.

Michael nodded. "Hire a property manager."

"Exactly," Steve said. "Own the business. Hire a business manager."

"One of my favorite examples is a company called Kabazzle," Steve said.

Michael leaned in.

"They use a private-label strategy," Steve continued. "Research products. You choose one. They handle branding, trademarks, manufacturing, shipping, and sales."

Michael's eyes widened. "Turnkey."

"Most products net $5–$15 per unit," Steve said.

"The target is to sell at least 1,000 units per month."

Michael did the math. "$5K to $15K per month."

"It takes a few months to ramp up," Steve said. "But the owner spends less than one hour per week on it. The rest is done by the management team."

"That cash flow can fund other investments," Steve said. "Diversification."

Michael nodded. "And then..."

"And then you sell the business," Steve continued. "Typically for three to four times earnings."

Michael smiled. "$360K to $480K on a $10K/month business."

Steve nodded. "With less than four hours a month of your time."

Steve continued, "Amazon U.S. sales exceed $400 billion annually."

Michael raised an eyebrow.

"Over 60% of that comes from small businesses," Steve said. "That's over $240 billion being earned by people just like you."

Michael exhaled slowly.

"And that doesn't include Walmart.com, TikTok, eBay, Shopify..."

"Or dozens of others," Steve finished.

As Albuquerque appeared ahead, Michael spoke quietly.

"So, a business can be the main thing you do–like Elon Musk or Jeff Bezos–or something you do part-time, or something that is managed for you? And business ownership isn't about being brilliant," he said.

"It's about structure, leverage, and execution."

Steve smiled. "And that's why it's the greatest wealth creator of all time."

MIKE'S WEALTH JOURNAL — Checkpoint 12 Reflections

- Business ownership has created wealth for centuries.

- Resources can be leveraged through OPM, OPK, and OPT.

- Starting point matters less than strategy and execution.

- Profitable businesses create cash flow and exits.

- Tax advantages amplify results.

- Ownership doesn't require daily involvement.

- Small businesses dominate massive markets.

CHAPTER 13:

UNDERSTAND THE #2 WEALTH CREATOR OF ALL TIME

Western New Mexico → Eastern Arizona (I-40 West)

The terrain shifted again as they crossed into Arizona.

Red earth. Long mesas. A different kind of permanence in the land — solid, unmoving, dependable.

Michael stared out the window.

"This feels... grounded."

Steve smiled. "Perfect place to talk about real estate."

"We just talked about business ownership," Steve said. "One of the two greatest wealth creators in history."

Michael nodded. "And real estate is the other?"

"Exactly," Steve said.

"First reason," Steve continued, "people like living indoors."

Michael laughed. "That helps."

"More than a third of Americans rent instead of own," Steve said. "Some choose to rent. Some can't qualify to buy. But they all need housing."

"And that number keeps climbing," Michael said.

"Because housing keeps getting more expensive," Steve replied. "Demand isn't going anywhere."

"Second," Steve said, "real estate appreciates."

Michael raised an eyebrow. "Even with crashes?"

"In the past hundred years," Steve said, "there have only been two periods where prices dropped nationally by more than 10%."

Michael listened closely.

"The Great Depression... and 2008," Steve continued. "Compare that to the stock market, which drops every 3.5 years on average."

Michael nodded slowly. "That's stability."

"Third," Steve said, "real estate produces monthly cash flow."

Michael smiled. "Rent checks."

"If you want financial freedom," Steve said, "you need passive cash flow. Few assets deliver it as consistently as real estate."

"Fourth benefit," Steve continued, "is leverage — using OPM."

Michael leaned in.

"Let's use a simple example," Steve said. "Completely made up — just to illustrate."

"Assume you buy a $200,000 house," Steve said.

"You put 20% down — that's $40,000."

Michael nodded.

"Assume your monthly cash flow is zero," Steve continued. "You apply everything toward the loan, paying it off in 20 years."

"And appreciation?" Michael asked.

"Use a conservative 4% annual appreciation," Steve said. "In 20 years, the house is worth over $425,000 and completely paid off. The OPM from the renters paid off the OPM from the bank mortgage."

Michael's eyebrows rose.

"Since your initial investment was just $40,000 and the asset is now worth over $425,000, that's an average annual return of over 12%," Steve said.

"Secured by a physical asset."

"The fifth benefit," Steve added, "is tax advantages."

Michael smiled. "Plural?"

"Many," Steve said. "Tax advantages when you buy. When you hold. When you earn income. When you sell."

Michael shook his head. "The tax code again."

"Written by wealthy people who own real estate," Steve said. "You should use it."

"So what does this look like in real life?" Michael asked.

Steve smiled. "BRRRR."

Michael laughed. "Sounds cold."

"Buy. Rehab. Rent. Refinance. Repeat," Steve said.

"You start by buying a distressed property," Steve explained.

"Not a shack — just outdated."

Michael nodded. "Old kitchen. Old floors. Paint."

"Exactly," Steve said. "You need to be able to add value to it."

"You rehab it," Steve continued. "Then you rent it."

Michael frowned. "Most people flip it here."

"And that's the mistake," Steve said.

"Yes, they get a short-term gain. However, they are paying a higher tax rate on that gain. More importantly, they do not get any long term cash flow. They are selling a goose that can provide cash flow forever."

"Once that property is cash-flowing," Steve said, "you refinance."

Michael smiled. "Pull the money back out."

"And repeat," Steve said.

"I've used this strategy dozens of times," Steve said.

"And helped clients use it hundreds more."

Michael leaned in.

"There's a company called Reilocity," Steve continued. "They guide investors through the entire BRRRR process."

"First," Steve said, "they identify a distressed property in a strong rental market."

Michael nodded.

"Second," Steve continued, "they connect you with a hard money or private lender."

"Assume they find you a property that costs $160K and the rehab cost is $40K. You need a total of $200K, but you do not need to use your own money for all of it."

Michael followed closely.

"You invest $50K," Steve said.

"The lender provides the other $150K."

"Third," Steve said, "Reilocity oversees the contractors during the rehab process."

Michael nodded.

"Fourth," Steve continued, "they connect you with a property manager who places tenants."

"Monthly income?" Michael asked.

"Anywhere from $1,200 to $5,000 per month," Steve replied.

"Now here's the key," Steve said.

Michael leaned in.

"After rehab," Steve continued, "the property appraises for $250K or more."

Michael smiled.

"With an 80% LTV loan," Steve said, "the bank lends $200K."

Michael's eyes widened. "You pay off the lender... and get your $50K back."

Steve nodded. "Your net investment cost is zero."

"You get your investment back and keep a house with $50K+ equity," Steve said.

"You also get monthly net cash flow of $500 to $1,500."

"And the icing on the cake...massive tax benefits."

Michael exhaled. "That compounds fast."

"The process takes four to six months," Steve said.

"That's two to three properties per year with the same $50K."

Michael did the math.

"What would you have after five years?" Steve continued.

Michael smiled. "10 to 15 houses. At $1,000 per house..."

"$10,000 to $15,000 per month," Steve finished.

"And rent rises with inflation... while your mortgage stays fixed for 30 years."

"Don't forget that each house will have at least $50,000 of equity because the lenders only loan 80% of their value. Take that times 10 to 15 properties. Even without factoring in appreciation, that is $500,000 to $750,000 of equity in those properties."

"And this," Steve said, "is just one real estate strategy."

Michael nodded. "Apartments. Storage. Land. Mobile homes."

"Exactly," Steve said.

As the Arizona desert stretched endlessly ahead, Michael spoke quietly.

"So real estate investing isn't about luck," he said.

"It's about structure, leverage, and repetition."

Steve smiled. "And that's why it's lasted for centuries."

MIKE'S WEALTH JOURNAL — Checkpoint 13 Reflections

- Real estate demand will never disappear.

- Appreciation is historically stable.

- Cash flow creates freedom.

- OPM multiplies returns safely when structured.

- BRRRR creates equity and income simultaneously.

- Refinancing recycles capital.

- Real estate scales with discipline and time.

CHAPTER 14:

IDENTIFY A PERFECT INVESTMENT

Central Arizona → Flagstaff, Arizona (I-40 West)

The elevation climbed as they pushed west.

The desert slowly gave way to pine trees. The air cooled. The road began to curve and rise — not sharply, but deliberately — as if the highway itself were asking for more precision.

Michael noticed it, too.

"This stretch feels different," he said. "Like the road demands more attention."

Steve nodded. "That's a perfect place to talk about Bullseye Investments."

"We just talked about the two greatest wealth creators of all time." Steve said, "You saw the power of owning a business and investing in real estate."

Michael nodded. "Either one could get you to financial freedom."

"And together?" Steve asked.

Michael smiled. "A lot faster."

"Exactly," Steve said. "But as your resources grow, something else becomes critical."

"You don't want all your wealth in one place," Steve continued. "You want diversification — but not random diversification."

Michael frowned. "So how do you choose?"

"That question," Steve said, "is why I created something I call the Bullseye Investment. I use it as a simple way to evaluate potential investments."

Steve continued, "You know what a Venn diagram is, right? Three circles and in the middle is the one spot where all three overlap."

Michael nodded. "Of course."

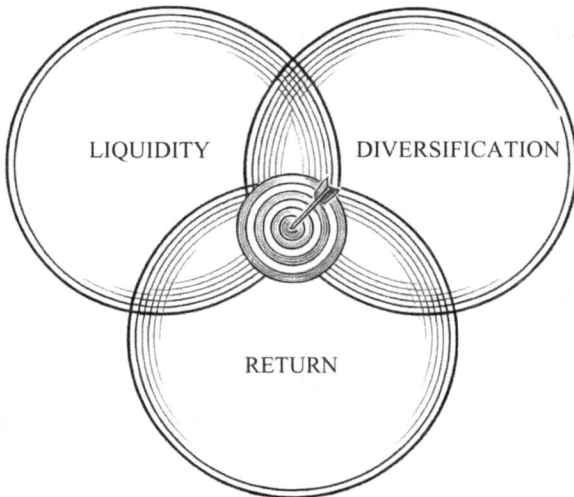

Liquidity - Gains available at least quartedly
Diversification - Not correlated to the stock market
Return - Goal of 4% per month

"When evaluating investments, I use three criteria and try to find opportunities that meet all three of them...the Bullseye in the middle." Steve said.

"First," Steve said, "liquidity."

Michael listened carefully.

"For me," Steve continued, "I want to pull out gains at least quarterly. Most of the investments allow withdrawals monthly or more often, quarterly is my minimum."

"And the principal?" Michael asked.

"I want the principal liquid within one year if needed," Steve said. "Again, Many are faster — daily, weekly or monthly – but one year is the minimum."

Michael nodded. "Different people, different needs."

"Exactly," Steve said.

"Second," Steve continued, "diversification."

Michael nodded.

"My wife and I already have significant exposure to the stock market through 401(k)s," Steve said. "So my priority is investments not tied to the stock market."

Michael smiled. "That makes sense."

"And your bullseye might look different," Steve added. "It depends on your portfolio."

"Third," Steve said, "return."

Michael raised an eyebrow. "Here it comes."

"My target return," Steve said calmly, "is 4% per month."

Michael laughed. "Seriously? That sounds crazy. Where do you find those?"

"Ten years ago, I would've thought that was crazy, too. We'll discuss where to find them in a bit." Steve said. "But stay with me."

Steve summarized:

"A bullseye investment for me is one that:

- Averages 4% per month, which is about 50% per year

- Is not tied to the stock market

- Provides liquidity at least quarterly"

Michael shook his head. "That's powerful."

"Before going further," Steve said, "let's slow down and look at returns."

Michael nodded.

"The S&P 500 has averaged about 12% per year over the past 50 years," Steve said.

Michael waited.

"You know me. I have always been a math nerd, so I have done the calculations and can tell you what a $10,000 investment would turn into over a six period." Steve continued.

- "At 12% per year or 1% per month, $10,000 turn into $20,000

- At 3% per month, $10,000 turns into $80,000

- At 4% per month, $10,000 turns into $160,000"

Michael exhaled slowly. "That's not incremental. That's exponential."

"You've heard about compounding," Steve said.

"The biggest factor in compounding?"

Michael answered quietly. "The rate of return."

Steve nodded. "Exactly. The difference between earning 3% per month and 4% per month may not sound like much, but over six years the investment earning 4% per month is worth twice as much."

Michael leaned forward.

"Okay. Where do you actually find 4% per month investments?"

Steve smiled. "I knew that was coming. First of all, it takes some work. I started off trying to find investments that earned 2% per month and then 3% per month and eventually my criteria increased to 4% per month."

"Second, your financial advisor isn't hiding them," Steve said.

"He's restricted."

Michael frowned. "By what?"

"Rules," Steve said. "They can only discuss registered securities approved by their broker-dealer. Remember, I was a financial advisor for nearly 10 years early in my career. I can tell you their compliance departments are pretty strict about that."

Steve continued:

"Is a rental property a good investment? Your financial advisor is prohibited from discussing it because it is not a registered security.

Bitcoin? — prohibited.

Private lending? — prohibited.

Should you own a business? — prohibited."

Michael shook his head. "That explains a lot."

"It makes sense," Steve said. "Years ago, I am sure some advisor gave advice on something that was not registered, the investor lost money and sued. The advisor and his broker-dealer had to spend money on legal fees to defend themselves on something they earned no commission on."

Michael nodded.

"So compliance just prohibits it," Steve said. "Most financial advisors probably wish they could discuss these other investments. They just can't."

"Would you expect a licensed realtor," Steve asked, "to advise you on stocks?"

Michael smiled. "Of course not."

"Same thing," Steve said.

"Most of the higher-return investments I've found," Steve continued, "are small, private opportunities."

Michael listened closely.

"Two of my favorites manage funds of $20-40 million each," Steve said.

Michael blinked. "That's small?"

"Compared to BlackRock or Vanguard managing $10 trillion?" Steve said. "Yes."

"They file something called a Regulation D exemption," Steve said.

Michael nodded.

"That means one of two things:

- Only accredited investors, or

- Completely private — no website, no ads, no social media"

"So you can't Google them," Michael said.

"Exactly," Steve replied. "You only find them by word of mouth."

"After I defined my criteria and knew what I was looking for," Steve said.

"I started asking around."

Michael smiled. "Simple."

"It took six months to find the first," Steve continued.

"That one led to three... those led to ten... and eventually I was in over 100 private opportunities."

Michael nodded. "So when you find one, you jump in?"

Steve laughed. "Not even close."

"Every investment has risk," Steve said.

- Some are scams

- Some underperform

- Some are wildly volatile

Michael listened carefully.

"You must understand both the actual risk and your risk tolerance."

"For smaller opportunities," Steve said, "that might include background checks."

Michael nodded.

"For all investments," Steve continued, "verify historical returns and volatility."

"Imagine two investments averaging 24% per year," Steve said.

"One earns 2% every month like clockwork," Michael said.

"And the other?" Steve asked.

"Big swings — up 20%, down 15%," Michael answered.

"Same average," Steve said. "Very different risk."

"Wow...I never thought of it that way. Two investments both averaging 24% a year could be completely different."

"Exactly." Steve continued, "Risk can also be broken down into actual risk and inherent risk. For example, my wife is very conservative."

Michael smiled. "I remember."

"She rejected several startups — until one was pharmaceutical," Steve said.

Michael laughed. "Because she is a pharmacist and understood it."

"Exactly," Steve said. "Familiarity reduced the perceived risk."

"Remember this rule," Steve said.

"Never invest unless you are an expert — or have a trusted advisor who is."

Michael nodded. "That keeps coming up."

"Yep. It is pretty important." Steve continued "It is important to understand your risk tolerance. I created a little example to help people think about their risk tolerance."

"Imagine ten startup companies you could invest in," Steve said. "You have $100,000 to invest and could invest $10,000 into each one. You know ahead of time that

- Two will fail and you will lose the money you invested in those two.

- Four stay flat and you break even on those.

- Two will double your investment

- Two will take off and increase your investment 10-fold

Michael's eyes widened.

"Of course, you do not know which companies will do what, so you invest in all ten," Steve said, "and you triple your money."

Michael nodded. "Some people love that."

"And some hate it," Steve said. "Some people look at that and say 'I would never invest money if there is a chance I could lose all my investment in two of the companies. You can use that example to think about your risk tolerance so you know which one you are."

"One last principle about risk," Steve said.

"The closer you are to the source, the stronger the investment."

"Gold futures are paper," Steve said.

"Gold coins are physical. I would take coins over paper any day."

Michael nodded.

"I once invested directly in a gold mine," Steve continued.

"Top gold-producing county in the US. 33,000 ounces per year — plus cash flow."

Michael smiled. "That's as close as it gets."

"You could own shares in a gas station," Steve said.

"Or the actual gas station.

Or the refinery.

Or the pipeline.

Or the oil well itself."

"Each step closer reduces risk," Michael said.

Steve nodded. "In general, yes. I am not saying that oil wells are always a safe investment. I am just saying that there will always be demand for resources like food, water, gold, and oil. The closer you are to owning the source that provides them, the better off you are."

Steve concluded:

"Let's return to the Bullseye Investments. Define your criteria.

Find investments that match.

Perform due diligence.

Manage risk."

Michael looked ahead as Flagstaff came into view.

"That's how you build a portfolio that lasts," he said.

"And that accelerates your financial freedom," Steve replied.

MIKE'S WEALTH JOURNAL — Checkpoint 14 Reflections

- Bullseye investments balance liquidity, diversification, and return
- Higher returns dramatically amplify compounding
- Advisors are limited by rules, not intent
- Private opportunities require relationships
- Due diligence is non-negotiable
- Understanding risk tolerance is crucial
- Being closer to the source strengthens investments

CHAPTER 15:

AVOID THE SCREE

Flagstaff → Kingman, Arizona (I-40 West)

They left Flagstaff behind under a pale morning sky, pines fading into open high desert again. The road fell into long, steady miles — the kind of drive where your thoughts start climbing whether you want them to or not.

Michael stared at the horizon.

"You've been talking about growing cash flow... building it, multiplying it, protecting it."

Steve nodded. "Today we talk about the thing that makes people feel like they're sliding backwards as much as they are climbing."

Michael frowned. "What's that?"

Steve smiled. "Taxes."

Steve paused, then said, "Have you ever heard the term scree?"

Michael blinked. "No."

Steve's voice shifted into story mode.

"Years ago, Katie and I were awakened at midnight to start the final climb to the summit of Mount Kilimanjaro so we could reach it around sunrise. We were at about 15,400 feet elevation, so the air was thin and it drained us. Even eating felt like work."

Michael listened closely.

"Despite being exhausted, under-nourished, and running on fumes," Steve continued, "we geared up anyway and started climbing."

"And?" Michael asked.

"That's when we learned about scree," Steve said. "It's like sand, but black, coarser. Every time you take a step up... your foot sinks in and slides back down. It's like climbing up a big sand dune."

Michael winced. "So you'd climb... and lose progress."

"Exactly," Steve said. "Big steps would slide back down and barely move you forward. It's demoralizing."

Michael nodded slowly. "How long did that last?"

"Hours," Steve said. "We hoped it would change quickly like the other terrain, but It didn't. Later we joked that they made us do it at night because if we'd seen how much we had to climb on the scree in daylight, we might've given up."

Michael exhaled. "Okay... I see where you're going."

Steve nodded. "That is exactly how I feel about taxes."

"You build passive cash flow," Steve said. "You feel momentum... enthusiasm... progress."

Michael nodded.

"And then taxes hit," Steve continued, "and a chunk of that progress gets wiped out. You slide backwards."

Michael sighed. "And the longer it goes, the more demoralizing it feels."

Steve nodded. "Exactly."

"But here's the good news," Steve said. "There are solutions. Every dollar you save in taxes is a dollar that can compound and accelerate your journey."

Michael sat up. "Okay. So what's the right way to think about this?"

"First," Steve said, "understand what tax planning is."

Michael listened.

"Congress created rules for how we calculate taxes," Steve said. "Tax planning is learning those rules and applying them so you can legally pay less."

Michael nodded. "Legally."

Steve's tone sharpened slightly.

"This is not trying to avoid taxes," Steve said. "That's tax evasion. That lands you in prison."

Michael held up a hand. "Not interested."

"And it's not trying to avoid paying your fair share," Steve continued. "It's about following the rules."

"And here's the part most people don't understand," Steve said. "Those rules were written to encourage behavior."

Michael frowned. "Like what?"

Steve smiled. "Let's have a quick history lesson."

"In the 1970s," Steve said, "the government realized there were a LOT of Baby Boomers and the system couldn't provide for everyone's retirement."

Michael nodded.

"So what did the government do?" Steve asked. "It created 401(k)s and offered tax deductions to encourage people to participate. Then IRAs with similar deductions."

Michael smiled. "So saving for retirement was literally incentivized."

"Exactly," Steve said.

"Then," Steve continued, "there were periods where dependence on foreign oil was a problem. Air quality deteriorated."

Michael nodded.

"So Congress offered tax breaks," Steve said.

"Solar panels in 1978.

Wind energy in 1992.

Electric vehicles in 1992."

Michael raised his eyebrows. "So tax planning is often doing what the government wants you to do."

Steve nodded. "That's why it's the opposite of un-American. If you are getting tax breaks, it is because you are doing something the government wants or needs you to do."

"Now," Steve said, "let's talk about a powerful strategy: layering."

Michael leaned in.

"It means controlling your tax rate by controlling where your income comes from," Steve said. "Imagine you're retired. The cash flow you use to pay your expenses is taxed in three ways."

Michael nodded.

"Some is taxed as income. That is the highest tax rate. Some is taxed as capital gains, which is lower. And some is tax-free."

Michael smiled. "Okay... layers."

"Assume you want to use $240,000 of income this year," Steve said.

Michael nodded.

"If it's all interest income," Steve continued, "it could be taxed as high as 32% depending on brackets and how you file."

Michael winced. "That's scree."

Steve nodded. "Now watch the alternative."

"What if you only take $95K as interest income," Steve said, "so the tax rate doesn't exceed 12% on that $95K?"

Michael nodded.

"And capital gains," Steve continued, "are 0% up to about $95K, so you can pull a lot from assets taxed as capital gains."

Michael did the math silently.

"And if you still need $50K," Steve said, "you use your assets that provide tax-free income."

Michael looked impressed.

"In scenario one," Steve said, "you pay $40K–$50K in taxes. In scenario two, you pay about $10K in taxes."

Michael exhaled. "Same income... totally different outcome."

"That," Steve said, "is tax layering. Not rocket science. But it requires planning. Most importantly, it gives you control."

Michael asked, "What are the common tax-free options?"

Steve nodded. "The most common: Roth IRAs and Roth 401(k)s."

Michael listened.

"Traditional IRAs and 401(k)s gave you a deduction upfront," Steve said. "Then growth is tax-deferred, but withdrawals are taxed later."

Michael nodded. "That's what most people do."

"In 1997," Steve said, "Congress introduced Roth rules."

Michael leaned in.

"No immediate deduction," Steve said, "but growth is deferred... and withdrawals in retirement can be TAX FREE."

Michael smiled. "So you're building future tax-free cash flow."

Steve nodded. "Many employer plans now offer Roth 401(k)s."

He added, "If possible — after consulting your tax advisor — I'd probably recommend stuffing as much money as you can into a Roth IRA or Roth 401(k)."

Michael said, "Most people plan to sell assets to create retirement income."

Steve nodded. "Mutual funds, real estate, gold, crypto... and they pay capital gains."

Michael shrugged. "Seems normal."

Steve's eyes stayed on the road.

"That's not what the wealthy do," he said.

Michael turned. "Okay... what do they do?"

"They own assets," Steve said. "Control assets. Keep assets."

Michael frowned. "So how do they pay bills if they never sell?"

Steve smiled. "They borrow against the asset."

Steve continued, "Remember the example earlier: $200K property, $40K down, $160K loan."

Michael nodded.

"Over 20 years, it grows to more than $425K," Steve said, "and the loan gets paid down."

Michael followed.

"If the house is paid off," Steve continued, "you could borrow with an 80% LTV and take out about $350K."

Michael's eyes widened. "And that borrowed money…"

"Is not taxed as income," Steve said. "Not taxed as capital gains. Because you didn't sell the house."

Michael smiled. "It's tax-free?"

"Absolutely. And you can do this with other assets," Steve said.

"Stocks?" Michael asked.

"Margin," Steve replied. "Borrow against your portfolio."

"Crypto?"

"You can borrow against crypto portfolios now."

"Gold?"

"There are outlets that lend using your gold as collateral," Steve said.

Michael nodded slowly. "And those loans are tax-free."

"Correct," Steve said.

Steve continued, "More than half of Americans have a life insurance policy."

Michael nodded. "Smart planning."

"But most people don't realize," Steve said, "you can borrow against it."

Michael raised his eyebrows. "Tax-free too?"

"Tax-free," Steve said. "And some provisions make it even better."

Michael leaned in.

"The interest rate on my policy loan is 4–5%," Steve said, "lower than most loans."

Michael nodded.

"And the best part?" Steve continued. "You don't have to repay it if you don't want to. The insurance company deducts the loan before paying the death benefit."

Michael blinked. "So it settles itself."

Steve nodded.

"Timing matters," Steve added. "Because policies need time to build cash value."

Michael listened.

"Get one when your family is young," Steve said. "Full protection if something happens."

"And later?" Michael asked.

"By the time kids are grown," Steve said, "the need for the death benefit is lower, and the cash value is higher. Borrowing reduces the death benefit, but it's often not detrimental if the kids don't need it."

Michael nodded. "That's strategic."

They drove in silence for a few miles. The road dipped and rose across the desert like a slow breath.

Then Steve said, "Let me tell you one more story — and my philosophy on taxes and prison."

Michael glanced over. "Uh-oh."

Steve nodded. "Years ago, I got a call from a financial planner in North Carolina."

Michael listened.

"He had a client named Michelle," Steve said. "Her mother had passed away a couple weeks earlier. Her dad had already passed away a couple years before."

Michael's expression softened.

"Michelle and her sister Missy were cleaning out the parents' house," Steve continued. "They also had a brother, Matt, but he was too lazy to help."

Michael smiled despite himself. "Of course he was."

Steve continued, "They opened a sock drawer... and found money. A lot of money."

Michael blinked. "How much?"

"$270,000 in cash," Steve said.

Michael sat up. "In a sock drawer?"

Steve nodded. "The advisor called because Michelle had two questions."

Michael leaned in. "Okay..."

"First," Steve said, "Do Missy and I have to share any of that with Matt?"

Michael laughed. "Ha! How did you answer that?"

Steve smiled. "Honestly? Whether they share it with him or not is none of my business."

Michael nodded.

"Then they asked the second question," Steve said, "How can I invest that money without paying taxes on it?"

Michael exhaled. "That sounds questionable."

Steve nodded. "Exactly."

Steve said quietly, "I'm always looking for ways to legally reduce taxes."

Michael nodded.

"But when in doubt," Steve continued, "I'd rather pay taxes than break the law."

Michael leaned back. "Agreed."

Steve smiled. "That led me to a saying I use a lot."

Michael waited.

"I do not want to be the richest person in my prison cell."

Michael laughed, then nodded seriously. "That's the line."

Steve looked ahead as Kingman approached in the distance.

"Taxes are scree," Steve said. "You can't avoid the mountain."

Michael nodded.

"But if you learn tax planning," Steve continued, "you stop sliding backward so much."

Michael smiled. "And the compounding gets stronger."

Steve nodded. "Exactly."

MIKE'S WEALTH JOURNAL — Checkpoint 15 Reflections

- Taxes can feel like climbing but sliding backward.

- Tax planning is legal strategy; tax evasion is prison.

- Congress uses tax incentives to guide behavior (401(k), IRA, solar, wind, EV).

- Layering income types can dramatically reduce taxes.

- Roth accounts create tax-free retirement income.

- The wealthy borrow against assets instead of selling them.

- Loans against real estate, stocks (margin), crypto, gold, and life insurance can be tax-free.

- "I do not want to be the richest person in a prison cell."

CHAPTER 16:

AUTOMATE YOUR WEALTH CREATION

Kingman, Arizona → Near the California Border (I-40 West)

The highway stretched out in front of them like a ribbon pulled tight across the desert.

No surprises. No twists. Just steady, relentless progress.

Michael watched the lane lines flash by in a rhythm that almost felt hypnotic.

"This road is... consistent," he said.

Steve nodded. "That's exactly the point."

Michael glanced over. "The point of what?"

Steve smiled. "The point of building wealth."

Steve continued, "Most people don't lose financially because they lack intelligence."

Michael raised an eyebrow.

"They lose because they get hijacked," Steve said. "By fear... or greed."

Michael nodded slowly. "I've felt both."

Steve pointed forward as if the road itself were illustrating the lesson.

"Picture this," Steve said.

"Oh no! My tech stock dropped 40% in the past week. I had better hurry and sell it before it goes any lower."

"That's fear."

Michael winced. "Yep."

Steve continued:

"Whoo-hoo! My tech stock is up 100% in the past month. I am going all-in and putting everything I have into this."

"That's greed."

Michael laughed once, then shook his head. "And that's how people get wrecked."

"Exactly," Steve said. "Way too many poor investing decisions have been made out of fear or greed."

Michael stared out the window. "I've missed opportunities because I was afraid to act... and I've also overcommitted when something was hot."

Steve nodded. "Most humans make terrible investing decisions — even though we like to think we're logical."

Michael smiled. "We're not."

"Fear and greed still drive the bus," Steve said.

Michael looked over. "So what's the fix?"

Steve said simply, "Don't rely on emotions."

Michael waited.

"Have computers do the work for you," Steve said. "Create systems that automate your investing... and accelerate your financial freedom."

Michael nodded. "Automatic."

Steve gestured to the highway. "Like this road. Consistent progress even when you're not thinking about it."

Steve continued, "It starts with the decision to invest money on a regular basis."

Michael nodded. "Okay."

"And what happens if you don't automate it?" Steve asked.

Michael smirked. "You tell yourself: 'Let's pay expenses this month and see if there's anything left over to invest.'"

Steve smiled. "And we both know how that ends."

Michael sighed. "There's never anything left."

"Or you find something more fun to do with it," Steve said. "And investing gets postponed."

"So automate it," Steve said.

Michael leaned in.

"That could mean your employer takes 401(k) deductions automatically," Steve continued.

"It could mean an automatic recurring transfer from your spending account to your investing account."

Michael nodded.

"I do both," Steve said. "One less decision. One more thing off the To-Do list. One step closer to financial freedom."

Michael smiled. "The system makes the decision."

"Exactly," Steve said.

Steve continued, "With my rental portfolio, I coordinated with my property manager so rent is automatically deposited into my investment bank account on the same day every month."

Michael's eyes widened. "So you don't even see it hit your spending account."

"I don't even have to think about it," Steve said.

Michael nodded slowly. "That's powerful."

"Set up different automations," Steve said, "so funds are always flowing into your Investment bank account."

Michael asked, "Once the money is there... then what?"

Steve smiled. "Continue the automation."

"One of the simplest examples is Dollar Cost Averaging," Steve said. "Many people already use it."

Michael nodded. "Investing the same amount, regularly, no matter what."

"In its simplest form," Steve continued, "you automatically invest the same amount into stocks on a schedule — regardless of what the stock is doing."

Steve gave him a clear example:

"Assume you invest $1,000 every month into a nice index fund."

Michael nodded.

"If the fund is $100 per share, you buy 10 shares."

Michael smiled. "Simple."

"If the price drops to $80," Steve said, "you don't panic. You invest the same $1,000... and now you buy about 12 shares instead of 10."

Michael's eyes lit up. "So the dip becomes a discount."

"Exactly," Steve said. "If you invest long-term, you expect it to rebound. Buying at $80 is an opportunity."

Steve continued, "Now imagine someone making a decision instead."

Michael nodded, already knowing where it was going.

"Last month shares were $100... now they're $80. That's a 20% drop.

Maybe I'll hold off this month and see what happens."

Steve looked at Michael. "That is a fear-based decision."

Michael nodded. "And they miss the discount."

"Dollar Cost Averaging prevents that," Steve said. "The system buys anyway."

Michael asked, "So money goes in automatically, and investing happens automatically."

Steve added "Many people do not realize that dollar cost averaging can be applied to many other investments, such as investing in crypto, gold, and more."

"Just set it and forget it." Steve continued. "Well...sort of."

Michael frowned. "Sort of?"

"It's good to check investment results sometimes," Steve said. "But not every few minutes. Not every few hours. Not even daily."

Michael smiled. "Guilty."

"I encourage you to look LESS often," Steve said. "Once a month or once a quarter. Checking less reduces stress."

Michael exhaled. "That would help a lot of people."

"But," Steve added, "you still need to review sometimes."

"So how do you do that without obsessing?" Michael asked.

"Simple," Steve said. "Set recurring reminders."

Michael nodded.

"I have a few," Steve continued.

"One of my larger investments reports the prior month's results on the 1st of every month. Withdrawals are only allowed in the first five days."

Michael raised an eyebrow. "So timing matters."

"Exactly," Steve said. "So I set a recurring reminder on the 1st to check the account, check the balance, and decide if I want or need a withdrawal."

Michael smiled. "Even that becomes automatic."

Steve continued, "As you diversify into different assets, you need a way to track them."

Michael nodded.

"Spreadsheet, app, system — doesn't matter," Steve said. "But you need to track each investment so you know the balance, cash flow, how it is performing relative to expectations and more."

Michael looked thoughtful. "Otherwise you're guessing."

"Right...and guessing is not very effective," Steve said.

Steve continued, "Imagine it's your scheduled review date."

Michael nodded.

"You open your tracker," Steve said. "You see Investment A made 10%

this year."

Michael asked, "Is that good or bad?"

Steve smiled. "That's the point. You can't answer unless you set expectations."

Michael nodded. "Because 10% could be amazing... or disappointing."

"Exactly," Steve said.

"If you earned 10% on a bank CD, you're incredible," Steve said. "If one of my Bullseye investments made 10% in a year, I'd be extremely disappointed."

Michael laughed. "Different ruler."

"That's why you need a KPI," Steve said. "Key Performance Indicator."

"For my favorite fund," Steve continued, "my KPI is a quarterly gain of 12%."

Michael nodded. "So each quarter you check performance."

"If it meets or exceeds the expectation," Steve said, "great."

"And if it doesn't?" Michael asked.

"I dive deeper," Steve said, "to see what happened... and whether it's expected to happen again. Is the failure to meet expectations a one-time event or is it a trend. Understanding that enables me to make a better decision on how to proceed."

They passed a sign that read "California State Line — 40 Miles", and

Michael smiled.

"Speaking of proceeding...We're getting close," he said.

Steve nodded. "Just not to the bridge yet."

Michael laughed. "Right — we've still got more checkpoints."

Steve said, "And these systems are what make the last miles easier."

Michael waited.

Steve finished:

"Use technology to automate investing. Establish KPIs. Create a tracker. When you do that, financial freedom stops being a 'hope'... or a 'possibility'..."

Michael nodded.

"And it becomes an inevitable destination," Steve said.

MIKE'S WEALTH JOURNAL — Checkpoint 16 Reflections

- Fear and greed cause most investing mistakes.

- Systems beat emotions; automation beats hesitation.

- Automate contributions (401k, transfers) before spending happens.

- Automate rental income deposits into the investment account.

- Dollar Cost Averaging prevents fear-based pauses and captures discounts.

- Check investments less often (monthly/quarterly) to reduce stress.

- Use calendar reminders for decision windows (like the 1st-of-month withdrawal window).

- Track every investment with balances and cash flow.

- Set KPIs so you know whether performance is good for that investment.

- Systems turn financial freedom from possibility into inevitability.

CHAPTER 17:

AVOID THE #1 OBSTACLE THAT PREVENTS SUCCESS

Crossing into California (I-40 West) → Mojave Desert Approach

A green sign flashed by on the right:

WELCOME TO CALIFORNIA

Michael sat up a little straighter. "We're in."

Steve nodded, eyes forward. "We are."

The desert didn't change much at first — still wide, still sun-bleached — but something about crossing that line made it feel like they were entering a new phase of the journey.

Michael stared at the sign disappearing behind them.

"It's strange," he said. "Crossing a border feels like progress."

Steve smiled. "It is."

Michael glanced over. "So what's the lesson for today?"

Steve didn't hesitate.

"The #1 obstacle."

Michael's face tightened. "Debt?"

Steve shook his head. "Not even close."

"Bad investments?" Michael asked.

Steve shook his head again.

Steve said calmly, "How you think."

Michael went quiet.

Steve continued, "This next statement might sound harsh, but it's true:

Your current financial status is the result of financial decisions you have made throughout your life."

Michael nodded slowly.

"If you're in a great financial position," Steve said, "congratulations. Keep it up."

Michael gave a small smile.

"But if you're struggling... or just unhappy with your financial situation," Steve continued, "then you need to re-evaluate how you think about money."

Michael looked down for a moment, then back to the road.

"Okay," he said quietly. "I'm listening."

Steve nodded. "Remember early stories — the lottery winners... and Grant Cardone?"

Michael nodded. "Same money, different outcome."

"Exactly," Steve said. "The goal is to help you think about money more like Grant Cardone does — to develop that wealthy mindset."

Michael breathed out. "So it starts in the head."

"It always starts in the head," Steve said.

"One of the most important mindsets," Steve continued, "is abundance."

Michael nodded.

"Too many people live with scarcity," Steve said. "They think there isn't enough money out there... that for one person to have more, someone else has to have less."

Michael stared through the windshield. "That's how most people talk."

Steve nodded. "But it's false."

He said plainly, "There are trillions and trillions of dollars out there — and more being printed all the time."

Michael smirked. "So the world isn't running out."

"No," Steve said. "There is an abundance of money."

Steve took a breath and said, "Many years ago, I was a consultant to financial advisors."

Michael turned slightly. He knew a story was coming.

"I remember two advisors who came to me around the same time," Steve said.

Michael nodded.

"The first one said:

'I made $100,000 last year. Can you help me increase that to $110,000 next year?'"

Michael clarified. "That is a 10% increase. Seems like a small but reasonable goal."

"Right." Steve said. "A small goal because he wasn't confident he could attract much more than what he already had. He had a scarcity mindset."

Steve continued.

"The second advisor came to me and said:

'I earned $200,000 last year. Can you help me earn $1 million this year?'"

Michael's eyebrows went up. "That's abundance."

"He knew the money was out there," Steve said. "He just needed help attracting more of it."

Michael asked, "So what happened?"

Steve smiled.

"With the first advisor, we made minor tweaks. He hit his goal and earned $112,000 the next year."

Michael nodded. "Good for him."

"With the second advisor," Steve continued, "we had to rethink his business model and make significant changes."

Michael leaned in.

"He missed his goal," Steve said, "and earned ONLY $920,000 that year."

Michael laughed. "Only."

Steve nodded. "And he easily passed a million the next year."

Michael looked forward. "So your goal shapes your strategy."

Steve said, "Right! Higher goals lead to strategies with higher outcomes."

Steve continued, "Another part of the abundance mindset is thinking both — while poor people think either/or."

Michael nodded. "Could you clarify that?"

Steve said, "Sure. A couple years ago, one of my investing clients was about to receive a $10,000 tax refund."

Michael listened.

"He asked me:

'Should I pay off my $10,000 credit card balance OR invest it?'"

Michael smiled. "I already know your answer."

Steve said, "Both."

Michael laughed.

"Invest it in a higher return asset that pays you every month," Steve said.

"Use those payments to pay off the credit card."

Michael nodded.

"Within a year," Steve continued, "his credit card was paid off... and he still owns the cash-flowing asset."

Michael's expression sharpened. "That's a wealth move."

Steve concluded that thought simply:

"In short: set higher goals... and create a strategy to achieve those goals."

Michael nodded. "That's abundance thinking."

Steve continued, "Next mindset is education."

Michael nodded.

"We already covered knowledge in the exponential formula," Steve said. "You should always be learning about money, investing, and financial management."

Michael exhaled. "Even if it's not my industry."

"Especially then," Steve said.

"You manage your income, expenses, and investments whether you're a doctor, teacher, software engineer — anything."

Michael nodded.

"And when I talk to successful people," Steve said, "every one of them can name at least five books they've read on investing and money management."

Michael smiled. "And they remember the nuggets."

"They can tell me a valuable nugget from each," Steve said.

Michael nodded.

"Set goals for how much time and money you'll dedicate to learning," Steve continued.

"Besides books, there are podcasts, workshops, courses, mentors and more."

Michael said quietly, "So education is part of the plan."

Steve nodded. "Always."

Steve continued, "The next Mindset is discipline."

Michael sighed. "The unsexy one."

Steve smiled. "The necessary one."

"Setting money aside requires discipline," Steve said, "and automations help."

"Making smart decisions requires discipline," he continued.

Then Steve said, "I remember an investor I spoke with a few years ago."

Michael listened.

"In our first conversation, he told me he tried an investment... didn't get expected results in the first month... so he moved the money somewhere else."

Michael frowned.

"Then moved it again... and again... and again," Steve said.

Michael shook his head. "Chasing."

"Shiny object syndrome," Steve said. "He lacked discipline to stick with any investment long enough to get results."

Steve said, "Another component of discipline is accountability."

Michael nodded.

"Say you commit to three steps next quarter," Steve said.

"Take a real estate investing course. Make your first real estate purchase. Automate deductions from your paycheck."

Michael nodded. "Good goals."

Steve asked, "Who holds you accountable?"

Michael went quiet.

"Who makes sure you don't procrastinate?" Steve continued.

"Or get distracted by the next shiny object?"

Michael sighed. "Nobody?"

Steve nodded. "Most respond in two ways."

"Some say, 'I hold myself accountable.' That sounds great, but it rarely works."

Michael nodded.

"Others say, 'My spouse is my accountability partner.' That sounds great too."

Michael smiled. "But..."

Steve said, "Is your spouse going to stand up to you and push you when you need it?"

Michael shook his head. "For most people... no."

Steve nodded.

"There are options," Steve continued.

"Investing circles with a friend or two. Online investing groups. Hiring a mentor."

Michael nodded.

"A good accountability coach," Steve said, "makes discipline much easier."

Steve continued, "Another mindset to adopt is the cash flow mindset."

Michael nodded. "Cash flow first."

"One way it shows up," Steve said, "is in purchases."

Michael listened.

"Wealthy people buy assets. Poor people buy liabilities."

Michael nodded. "Could you define that?"

Steve said:

"An asset increases in value and/or generates cash flow."

"Gold is an asset that should increase over time."

"A rental property should increase in value AND generate cash flow."

Michael nodded.

"A liability decreases in value and doesn't generate income," Steve continued.

"One example is a new boat."

"Designer clothes."

Michael smiled. "Ouch."

Steve continued, "Put another way: if you buy $5,000 of designer clothes on a payment plan..."

Michael nodded.

"Not an asset," Steve said. "Negative cash flow. Another expense you must cover."

Michael exhaled. "That's the trap."

Steve's tone shifted. "The last mindset is action."

Michael sat up.

"Remember," Steve said, "these last few days have not been just for me to entertain you. This information is a guideline to change your life... but ONLY if you take action."

Michael smiled. "I won't just treat it like Netflix binge. Instead of walking away thinking 'That was entertaining' I will act on the information you provided."

Steve nodded. "Good!"

Michael nodded. "So what makes people take action?"

Steve said, "Motivation."

"'Being wealthy sounds nice' is not motivating enough," Steve said.

"'So I don't have to work' isn't a great answer either."

Michael nodded.

Steve continued, "My initial motivation that made the difference was making sure I had enough cash flow to put both of my kids through college."

Michael's face softened.

"Family is my top priority," Steve said. "I named my real estate business after my wife and kids."

Michael nodded.

"And every time I do anything with that business — several times a day — I'm reminded of why I run it."

Michael said quietly, "That's powerful."

Steve continued, "My wife and I love to travel and explore. That's when we're happiest."

Michael smiled.

"And from my parents," Steve said, "I inherited the desire to help those in need."

Michael nodded.

"So my motivation is this:

'To happily explore the world with my soulmate while also making the world a better place.'"

Michael stared at the road. "That's a real why."

"Determine your real motivation," Steve said.

"It may not sound necessary, but wanting financial independence for years made no difference for me."

Michael listened.

"It wasn't until I found my why that things started to change."

Steve paused and said, "Earl Nightingale had a quote I love."

Michael turned slightly.

"He compared motivation to a pie recipe," Steve said.

"A woman who is not thinking about making a pie doesn't need a recipe or ingredients."

Michael smiled.

"It isn't until she wants it bad enough to take action that the mind organizes the steps."

Michael nodded slowly.

Steve said, "Think of financial freedom as your pie."

Michael smiled. "Everybody wants pie."

Steve laughed. "Exactly."

"Everyone would accept financial freedom if it fell from the sky," Steve said. "But we know how that ends for lottery winners."

Michael nodded.

"When your mindset shifts from wanting financial freedom to being motivated to create it," Steve continued, "that's when your mind goes to work. It helps you create your recipe, gather ingredients, and make it happen."

Michael exhaled. "That's mindset."

Steve said, "You will never accidentally end up at financial freedom."

Michael nodded.

"I compare it to summiting Mount Kilimanjaro," Steve continued.

Michael smiled. "Back to the mountain."

"My wife and I committed to doing it years ago," Steve said.

"Once we committed, we researched how."

Michael nodded.

"We had to arrange travel logistics, get a guide, acquire gear, and train."

Michael said, "You didn't just wander onto the summit."

Steve smiled. "There's no way we would have accidentally ended up at the top."

"It happened because we made a commitment... then figured out what it would take."

Michael nodded slowly. "Financial freedom is the same."

"You'll never accidentally get there," Steve said. "But if you make a mental commitment... you can."

Michael looked ahead as the California desert opened wider.

"And probably faster than you think," Steve added.

Michael smiled — not a big smile, but a steady one.

"Then I'm committing," he said. "For real."

Steve nodded once. "Good. Because commitment is the moment the map becomes real."

MIKE'S WEALTH JOURNAL — Checkpoint 17 Reflections

- My current financial position came from my decisions — so I can make new ones.

- Abundance mindset: money is abundant; set bigger goals and build strategies to match.

- Scarcity vs abundance example: $100K → $112K with tweaks; $200K → $920K with a rebuilt model.

- Wealthy people think "both," not "either/or" (the $10K refund strategy).

- Education mindset: learn money skills no matter your profession; books, podcasts, mentors, courses.

- Discipline matters; avoid shiny object investing.

- Accountability is often missing; spouse/self usually isn't enough — use circles, groups, mentors.

- Cash flow mindset: buy assets, not liabilities (designer clothes on payment plans = negative cash flow).

- Action mindset: motivation is required; "find your why."

- You never accidentally reach financial freedom — you commit, then execute.

CHAPTER 18:

TAKE THE NEXT STEP

Arrival: San Francisco → The Golden Gate Bridge

The fog rolled in slowly.

Not the thick, blinding kind — just enough to soften the edges of the city as Steve guided the car toward the final rise. The red towers of the Golden Gate Bridge emerged ahead of them, massive and unmistakable, stretching across the water like a promise kept.

Michael leaned forward, resting his forearms on his knees.

"We made it," he said quietly.

Steve nodded. "We did."

They pulled over at a scenic overlook just before the bridge. The engine clicked softly as it cooled. Steve shut off the ignition, and for a moment neither of them moved.

Then they stepped out of the car.

The wind was cool and steady, carrying the distant hum of traffic and the salt of the bay. The city stretched out below them — alive, busy, relentless. Cars streamed past on the bridge, people heading somewhere — some chasing deadlines, some chasing dreams. Everyone moving along one of the Levels of Financial Freedom, though most had no idea where they were or how to change course.

Michael broke the silence.

"That's a lot," he said. "Everything you shared on this trip."

Steve smiled slightly. "It is."

Michael shook his head slowly.

"Levels. Cash flow. Mindset. Time. Knowledge. Other people's money, time, and expertise. Strategies stacked on top of strategies."

Steve leaned back against the car. "Then don't rush it."

Michael looked over.

"Let it sink in," Steve continued. "Re-read what you wrote in your journal. Think about it. But don't do the one thing that kills more dreams than failure ever could."

Michael already knew the answer.

"Don't put it down and walk away."

Steve nodded. "Exactly."

Steve gestured back toward the road they had traveled.

"Before any journey," he said, "you need to know where you're starting."

Michael nodded.

"So the first thing you do," Steve continued, "is identify which of the Five Levels of Financial Freedom you're on right now."

Michael exhaled. "No ego. No shame. Just honesty."

"Exactly," Steve said. "You can't plan the next step if you don't know your current position."

Steve shifted his weight, looking out toward the bridge.

"Next question," he said. "Who's helping you move forward?"

Michael frowned slightly. "You mean... besides you?"

Steve smiled. "I mean in your real life.

A mentor. A coach. An accountability partner. An investing group. A mastermind."

Michael thought about it. "I've mostly tried to do everything on my own."

Steve nodded. "Most people do. And most people stall because of it."

Steve continued calmly, methodically — the same way he had guided the entire trip.

"Now take inventory."

Michael listened.

"What knowledge do you already have?" Steve asked.

"What Other People's Knowledge do the people around you have?"

Michael nodded.

"What knowledge do you still need?" Steve continued.

"And who needs to be added to your team?"

Michael glanced back toward the bridge.

Steve kept going.

"How much money do you have to work with right now?

How much access do you have to Other People's Money?"

Michael nodded slowly.

"How much time can you realistically dedicate to building wealth?

And how much Other People's Time can you leverage?"

Michael smiled faintly. "I never thought about time that way before."

"Most people don't," Steve said. "That's why they stay stuck."

Steve turned and pointed toward the city.

"Look at your investments," he said.

"Are you using business ownership to create wealth?

Have you started building real estate?

Are your other investments diversified and producing passive cash flow?"

Michael nodded.

"What are your criteria for a Bullseye Investment?" Steve asked.

"And how are you going to find more of them?"

Michael laughed softly. "That question would've overwhelmed me a week ago."

Steve smiled. "Now it excites you."

Steve finally turned fully toward Michael.

"But here's the most important question of all."

Michael met his eyes.

"What action are you going to take in the next 24 hours?"

Michael didn't answer right away.

Steve added, "And just as important — who's going to make sure you actually do it?"

Michael exhaled slowly.

"If I can't answer that second question..."

Steve finished it for him.

"Find an accountability partner immediately."

Michael nodded. "I get it now."

Steve glanced at his watch, then back at Michael.

"I've got to head to the airport soon," he said quietly.

Michael nodded. He knew what that meant. Steve would fly back to North Carolina. He would take the final leg alone.

Steve reached into the car and handed Michael his worn leather journal — the one he'd filled with notes, questions, realizations, and moments of clarity during hundreds of miles of the journey.

"Keep this close," Steve said. "You didn't just write ideas in here. You rewired how you think."

Michael flipped through a few pages, smiling softly.

"I'm not the same guy who showed up at your place on the beach," he said.

Steve smiled. "No. You're not."

Steve took a step back and gestured toward the driver's seat.

"Alright," he said. "It's your turn to drive again."

Michael paused.

"But this time," Steve continued, "you're not just driving a car. You're driving your future. Same road. Same responsibilities. Completely different mindset."

Michael nodded, understanding the weight of it.

"You know where you're going now," Steve added. "And more importantly, you know how to stay on the road."

They shook hands — not rushed, not sentimental, just solid.

A short time later, Michael stood curbside in a quiet Bay Area neighborhood, handing his son the keys.

The car had reached its destination.

His son smiled. "So... how was the trip?"

Michael looked at him for a moment, then nodded.

"It was great," he said. "We'll talk about it over dinner. Those big dreams you've been talking about? I finally understand the roadmap for how we can actually make them happen."

They got into the car and drove away — moving forward with clarity, intention, and a future that finally felt navigable.

MIKE'S WEALTH JOURNAL — Final Reflections

- I must identify my current level before choosing my next step.

- Financial freedom requires a team — mentors, accountability, and community.

- I must assess my true resources: Knowledge, Time, Money — and leverage OPK, OPT, and OPM.

- Wealth accelerates when business ownership, real estate, and diversified cash-flowing assets work together.

- Clear criteria (Bullseye Investments) guide smart decisions.

- Action within 24 hours matters more than intention.

- Accountability turns commitment into momentum.

- Financial freedom is not an accident — it is a decision followed by disciplined action.

ABOUT THE AUTHOR

Steve Lawson knows firsthand that earning more money doesn't guarantee financial success.

Raised below the poverty line up to age twelve and spending his early childhood in foster care, Steve didn't grow up with financial advantages—or financial education. What he did develop was discipline, resilience, and a deep curiosity about how money really works.

That curiosity led him to Indiana University, where he studied Accounting and Finance, and eventually into a career in traditional financial planning. In his early years, Steve followed—and taught—the conventional wisdom most people receive: save diligently, invest conservatively, and hope the market cooperates.

Then reality intervened. The dot-com crash, years of underwhelming results, and watching "safe" strategies fail too many people forced Steve to question everything he believed about wealth. He began studying how financial independence was actually created—not in theory, but in practice—through real estate, business ownership, cash flow, leverage, and mindset rather than outdated formulas and guesswork.

Ironically, while Steve spent years helping others build wealth, he delayed applying those same principles to his own life. That changed in 2018. With two children approaching college age and time running short, he committed to building enough passive cash flow to fund their education and secure his family's future.

What followed exceeded every expectation. In less than two years, Steve generated over $30,000 per month in passive income—without relying solely on the stock market. That success became the foundation for his unconventional approach: wealth built on cash flow, leverage, automation, and diversification rather than income, job titles, or arbitrary "magic numbers."

Today, Steve teaches others how to follow a similar path—regardless of their background, income level, or starting point. His work challenges traditional financial thinking and replaces it with a practical, empowering roadmap designed for real life.

Steve believes financial freedom isn't about getting rich for its own sake. It's about having the ability to do what you love, with the people you love, on your own terms.

www.ingramcontent.com/pod-product-compliance
Lightning Source LLC
Chambersburg PA
CBHW071234210326
41597CB00016B/2051